TIMELESS
Trivia

Volume Nine

Volume Nine

Music of the 21st Century Edition

1000 Questions, Stumpers, and Teasers
about the Music We Love

by

BOB HAMMITT

Edited by

DUELLA SCOTT-HULL

From the Author

Thank you for your purchase of "Timeless Trivia Volume Nine: Music of the 21st Century." We hope that it brings you learning, smiles, fun and memories.

The "Timeless Trivia" series began during the early stages of the Covid-19 pandemic. In order to provide friends and family with a way to stay connected and pass the time, I would do nightly trivia contests on Instagram live. By doing this, I amassed a large number of questions. After a few friends asked me for copies of the questions, I decided to turn them into a book, which became the first volume of the "Timeless Trivia" series.

The book received such positive reviews, we decided to do more. Three years later, here is our ninth volume, putting the finishing touches on three volumes based solely on music trivia. The next three will each be on sports trivia of different eras.

Please support Timeless Trivia by leaving us a rating and review on Amazon, and by sharing our books on your own social media pages. If this is your first purchase of a Timeless Trivia book, there are eight more available on Amazon!

Thanks again for your purchase of this volume. We hope you enjoy it!

Sincerely,

Bob Hammitt

1. Whose album "1989", released in 2014 is her best-selling of all time?

2. Name the former host of "American Top 40" who was also the voice of Shaggy from Scooby Doo, and passed away in 2014.

3. What band topped the album charts in both America and the United Kingdom in 2005 with their third album "X and Y"?

4. Who, in 2017, became the first rapper inducted into the songwriter's hall of fame?

5. Marc Anthony and what music superstar divorced in 2014?

6. With what song did South Korean rapper Psy top the music charts in over 30 countries with in 2012?

7. What band had a number one hit in the U.S. in 2000 with "Everything You Want?

Answers

1) Taylor Swift
3) Coldplay
5) Jennifer Lopez
7) Vertical Horizon

2) Casey Kasem
4) Jay-Z
6) "Gangnam Style" *

*The video for "Gangnam Style" was the first video to be uploaded over one billion times on YouTube.

8. In 2008, Billy Joel played the final concert ever held at what New York City Stadium?

9. Who had a top ten country hit with the single "Johnny Cash" off his 2007 album, "Relentless"?

10. What artist scored their first number one hit in the United States in 2020 with "Watermelon Sugar"?

11. What is the name of the lead singer of the band "The Cars" who passed away in 2019?

12. Who, in 2007, became the youngest artist to write, produce, and perform a number one hit with "Crank That"?

13. What band's "Songs of Innocence" was given freely to everyone who had an iTunes account in 2014?

14. What band had their first number on album in 2000 with "Kid A"?

Answers

8) Shea Stadium

9) Jason Aldean

10) Harry Styles

11) Ric Ocasek

12) Soulja Boy*

13) U2

14) Radiohead

Previously, the youngest artist to accomplish this feat had been Debbie Gibson, with her 1987 hit "Foolish Beat."

15. On March 25, 2022, Taylor Hawkins was found dead in his hotel room. What band did he serve as a longtime drummer for?

16. What is the name of the 2009 hit by Lady Gaga which begins with "I wanna hold 'em like they do in Texas, please fold 'em, let 'em hit me, raise it, baby stay with me"?

17. Who paired with Jay-Z on the 2002 hit "Bonnie and Clyde"?

18. Who won the Country Music Association's award for album of the year in 2012 with "Chief"?

19. What band had a top five hit with their 2014 release "Shut Up and Dance"?

20. What rock legend tied a record by winning in eight categories at the Grammy Awards in the year 2000?

21. What Canadian rapper and singer gained his initial fame by playing the character of Jimmy Brooks on the CTV teen drama, "Degrassi: The Next Generation"?

Answers

15) Foo Fighters

16) "Poker Face"

17) Beyonce

18) Eric Church

19) Walk the Moon*

20) Carlos Santana

21) Drake

*The song spent 27 weeks on top of Billboard's "Hot Rock Songs" chart, breaking a record for longevity previously shared by Hozier and Imagine Dragons.

22. What is the title of the 2005 chart topping hit by Carrie Underwood which begins with "Right now, he's probably slow dancin' with a bleach-blond tramp and she's probably gettin' frisky"?

23. Name the 21st century superstar who was born April 27, 1988, with the name Melissa Viviane Jefferson.

24. What Lil Wayne song was certified by the RIAA as the best-selling ringtone in history?

25. Name the lead singer of Hootie and the Blowfish who began his first tour as a solo country music artist in 2009.

26. Name the popular song by My Chemical Romance from 2006 which begins with "When I was a young boy, my father took me into the city to see a marching band."

27. Who set a record for most Grammy nominations for a rapper with his 2015 album "To Pimp a Butterfly"?

28. Who, in 2016 became the first woman to win the Grammy for album of the year a third time?

Answers

22) "Before He Cheats" 23) Lizzo
24) "Lollipop" 25) Darius Rucker
26) "Welcome to the Black Parade" 27) Kendrick Lamar
28) Taylor Swift*

Three males have won the award three times: Frank Sinatra, Paul Simon, and Stevie Wonder.

29. Whose song "Be Without You" set a record for most consecutive weeks on top of the R and B chart in 2006?

30. What punk band had their first ever number one album in 2004 with "American Idiot"?

31. What rapper famously said "George Bush doesn't care about black people" during a live telecast of a Hurricane Katrina relief effort?

32. What music superstar appeared on the season premiere of "CSI: Crime Scene Investigation" in 2010 as a serial bomber?

33. Name the popular electronic dance music duo consisting of Redfoo and Sky Blue.

34. What British indie rock and folk band had their most popular hit in 2008 with "5 Years Time"?

35. Name the legendary singer who was the first female inducted into the Rock and Roll Hall of Fame who died from pancreatic cancer in 2018.

Answers

29) Mary J. Blige
31) Kanye West
33) LMFAO *
35) Aretha Franklin

30) Green Day
32) Justin Bieber
34) Noah and the Whale

Redfoo is the youngest son of Motown Records founder Berry Gordy. Sky Blue is Gordy's grandson.

36. What country superstar announced their divorce from producer "Mutt" Lange in 2008?

37. Justin Timberlake had his fifth number one single in 2016 with "Can't Stop The Feeling!" What movie soundtrack was it from?

38. Who, at age 65, became the oldest living person to enter Billboard's Album chart in the top spot with his "Modern Times" in 2006?

39. Whose 2001 album "Take Off Your Pants and Jacket" was the first ever punk rock album to debut at number one on the Billboard albums chart?

40. Who, in 2021, became the second female rapper in history to win the Grammy for Best New Artist?

41. Who played what was billed to be his final concert ever in Arlington, Texas on June 7, 2014, which was the largest indoor concert in the history of North America?

42. What British band's debut album "Whatever People Say I Am, That's What I'm Not," was the fastest selling debut album in the history of the U.K.?

Answers

36) Shania Twain*

37) "Trolls"

38) Bob Dylan

39) Blink 182

40) Megan Thee Stallion

41) George Strait

42) Arctic Monkeys

*Lange had been having an affair with Twain's friend and assistant Marie-Anne Thiebaud. Later, Lange would marry Thiebaud, and Twain would marry Thiebaud's ex-husband Frederic Thiebaud.

43. Who, in 2020, became the first non-English language act to be Spotify's most streamed artist of the year?

44. What is the name of the single released by Eminem in November 2000 about an obsessed fan, which went to number one in 12 countries?

45. What music superstar married her childhood friend, Jason Alexander, in Las Vegas in 2004, a marriage that lasted only 55 hours?

46. Name the legendary music producer who died in prison of coronavirus in 2021, where he was serving time for killing actress Lana Clarkson in 2003.

47. Whose 2002 album "A Rush of Blood to the Head" was ranked at number 324 on Rolling Stone Magazine's list of the 500 greatest albums of all time?

48. Who had their first number one country hit in 2008 with "Chicken Fried"?

49. Whose theme song to the 2012 James Bond movie "Skyfall" won the Academy Award for Best Original Song?

Answers

43) Bad Bunny

44) "Stan" *

45) Britney Spears

46) Phil Spector

47) Coldplay

48) Zac Brown Band

49) Adele

In 2017 the Oxford American Dictionary defined the word "Stan" as "An overzealous or obsessive fan of a particular celebrity."

50. In 2005, who became the first woman to have her "MTV Unplugged" album debut at number one?

51. Who was named by Billboard Magazine as the top female Latin artist of the decade for both the 2000s and the 2010s?

52. After a 2012 trip to Jamaica, Snoop Dogg announced that he would now go by what name?

53. Who performed her hits "I Kissed a Girl," "California Gurls," and "Teenage Dream" at halftime of the 2015 Super Bowl?

54. Whitney Houston appeared in her last film in the 2012 movie "Sparkle," What singer and former American Idol winner played Houston's daughter?

55. Who won the Grammy for "Best Rock Album" in 2003 for "The Rising"?

56. What rapper did former Destiny's Child member Kelly Rowland team with to have a number one hit with "Dilemma" in 2002?

Answers

50) Alicia Keys

51) Shakira

52) Snoop Lion

53) Katy Perry *

54) Jordin Sparks

55) Bruce Springsteen

56) Nelly

Perry's Super Bowl half time appearance was the most watched in history, until she was surpassed by Rihanna in 2023.

57. On December 13, 2013, Rebecca Black paired with Dave Days to release a follow up to her hit single "Friday." What was it called?

58. Ten people were crushed to death in November of 2021 at a Houston concert festival known as "Astroworld." What rapper founded the event?

59. Who won the Academy of Country Music's award for "Song of the Year" for his 2001 release "Where Were You (When the World Stopped Turning)"?

60. What is the title of the 2008 chart topping hit by Pink which begins with the lyrics "I guess I just lost my husband; I don't know where he went. So, I'm gonna drink my money, I'm not gonna pay his rent"?

61. Whose second album, titled "The Thrill of it All" debuted at number one on the album charts in both the U.S. and U.K. in 2017?

62. What popular 21st century band is comprised of three brothers named Nathan, Jared, and Caleb Followill and their cousin Matthew Followill?

63. What country music star teamed with Lil Nas X on his 2019 remix of "Old Town Road"?

Answers

57) "Saturday"
59) Alan Jackson
61) Sam Smith
63) Billy Ray Cyrus*

58) Travis Scott
60) "So What"
62) Kings of Leon

*In April 2019, the song broke the record for most streams in a week. The previous record was held by Drake's "In My Feelings."

64. The daughter of Beyonce and Jay Z made history in 2020 by becoming the youngest person ever to win a B.E.T. award, at the age of eight. What is her name?

65. What rock legend released his 26th studio album "Blackstar," on January 8, 2016, which was his 69th birthday, then died two days later of liver cancer.

66. What is the title of the 2004 movie in which the title character dances in a famous scene to the song "Canned Heat" by the British band Jamiroquai?

67. What band had their first number one album in 2006 with their ninth album "Stadium Arcadium"?

68. What is the name of the all-girl south Korean group who made their debut in 2016 with their album "Square One"?

69. Who had a number one hit in 2012 with "Call Me Maybe"?

70. The Weeknd won the Grammy for Best R and B performance for his 2015 release "Earned It." What movie soundtrack was the song from?

Answers

64) Blue Ivy Carter

65) David Bowie

66) "Napolean Dynamite"

67) Red Hot Chili Peppers

68) Blackpink

69) Carly Rae Jepsen*

70) "50 Shades of Grey"

*"Call Me Maybe" is only the second song by someone named Carly to reach the top spot on the chart. The first: "You're So Vain" by Carly Simon.

71. Name the American indie band whose songs include "Skinny Love" and "Blood Bank" which takes its name from the French phrase meaning "Good Winter."

72. What country music star did Garth Brooks propose to in 2005?

73. What is the successful rapper, actor, and businessman who was born as Curtis James Jackson III better known as?

74. Name the music and acting superstar who began her career on the television series "Barney and Friends" in 2002.

75. What Australian band had their first top 40 hit in the U.S. in 2003 with "Are You Gonna Be My Girl"?

76. Whose 2012 release "Babel" was awarded the Grammy for Album of the Year?

77. Whose second studio album "Kirk" debuted at number one on the U.S. Billboard 200 in 2019?

Answers

71) Bon Iver

72) Trisha Yearwood

73) 50 Cent*

74) Selena Gomez

75) Jet

76) Mumford and Sons

77) Da Baby

*50 Cent has had one of the longest running rivalries in rap music with Ja Rule. Amongst the many slights the two have taken towards the other, 50 Cent once bought up the first 200 seats at a Ja Rule concert just so he could leave them empty.

78. Name the one hit wonder who won the Grammy for Best Dance Recording at the 2001 Grammy awards for "Who Let the Dogs Out."

79. Who, in 2018, became the first woman to win an Academy Award, BAFTA, Golden Globe, and Grammy in one year?

80. Name the song by Meghan Trainor which stayed at number one for eight weeks in 2014.

81. What is the title of the popular series on MTV, which made its debut in the year 2000, showing the homes of Jewel, Moby, and the Osbournes in its first episode.

82. Who caused a controversy in 2010 when he referred to Jessica Simpson as "sexual napalm" in an interview with Playboy Magazine?

83. Whose album "Back to Black" became the best-selling album in the history of the U.K. after she died of alcohol poisoning in 2011?

84. Name the country music singer who had his recording contract suspended in 2021, despite having the number one country album in America at the time, after a video of him using racial slurs surfaced.

Answers

78) Baha Men

79) Lady Gaga

80) "All About That Bass"

81) "MTV Cribs"

82) John Mayer

83) Amy Winehouse

84) Morgan Wallen*

*In 2020, Wallen was pulled from an appearance from Saturday Night Live days before the show due to a video surfacing of him violating Covid-19 protocols by partying maskless and kissing several women.

85. Layne Staley was discovered dead in his Seattle apartment on April 19, 2002.What grunge band was he the lead singer of?

86. Who had a top ten album in 2000 with his debut album, released when he was 13, titled "Beware of Dog"?

87. Who won the Academy of Country Music's entertainer of the year award each year from 2006 to 2008?

88. What is the duo of CeeLo Green and Danger Mouse better known as?

89. Who, in 2019, became the first boy band to have number one albums in three different decades?

90. What country music star did Gwen Stefani marry in 2021?

91. What 2011 hit by Foster the People begins with the lyrics "Robert's got a quick hand. He'll look around the room but won't tell you his plan"?

Answers

85) Alice in Chains

86) Lil Bow Wow

87) Kenny Chesney

88) Gnarls Barkley

89) Backstreet Boys

90) Blake Shelton

91) "Pumped Up Kicks" *

The song was about a high school student plotting revenge against kids who had bullied him. "Pumped Up Kicks" is a reference to Reebok Pumps, a popular shoe model often worn by affluent teenagers at the time.

92. Fred Durst has been the lead vocalist for what hard rock band since 1994?

93. Who became the first rapper to win trophies for both Best Song and Best Record at the 2019 Grammy Awards?

94. Who rose to fame while playing the character Cat Valentine in the Nickelodeon series "Victorious" from 2010 to 2013?

95. Who had their second number one album in 2013 with "Save Rock and Roll"?

96. What is the title of the 2003 Toby Keith song which begins with "American girls and American guys, we'll always stand up and salute, we'll always recognize"?

97. Name the song by Pharrell Williams released November 21, 2013, which would later be named the Billboard song of the year in 2014.

98. In 2003, 100 people were killed and 230 injured when a fire broke out at the Station Night Club in Rhode Island while what band was playing?

Answers

92) Limp Bizkit   93) Childish Gambino
94) Ariana Grande   95) Fall Out Boy*
96) "Courtesy of the Red, White, and Blue"   97) "Happy"
98) Great White

*Fall Out Boy got their name during their second show when it asked the crowd what their name should be. An audience member shouted out "Fall Out Boy," a fictional superhero from the animated series "The Simpsons."

99. Whose 2000 album "Hybrid Theory" is, as of 2023, the best-selling rock album of the 21st century?

100. Whose 2005 single "You're Beautiful" reached number one in both the United States and United Kingdom?

101. With an estimated worth of $1.7 billion, who did Forbes Magazine label as the richest female singer in the world in 2021?

102. In 2002, Widespread Panic headlined the first of what musical festival now annually held on a farm in Manchester, Tennessee?

103. What band set a record, which would later be broken, for highest grossing tour in history with their "A Bigger Bang" tour, which began in 2005?

104. Who had their fourth number one song in 2019 with "Circles"?

105. What Canadian singer-songwriter released their 14th and final album titled "You Want it Darker" in 2016, just 17 days before his death?

Answers

99) Linkin Park

100) James Blunt

101) Rihanna*

102) Bonnaroo

103) The Rolling Stones

104) Post Malone

105) Leonard Cohen

*According to Forbes, Rihanna trails only Oprah Winfrey as the richest female entertainer in the world.

106. Whose 2015 song "Stressed Out" became the first song to reach a billion streams on Spotify?

107. What boy band's "Where We Are" tour was the highest grossing tour of 2014?

108. Whose song "Where Is the Love" was the best-selling song in the U.K. in 2003?

109. What rapper was convicted of shooting Megan Thee Stallion in December 2022?

110. What Christmas song reached the top of the U.S. Billboard chart in 2019, 25 years after it was released?

111. Members of the all-female band "Pussy Riot" were arrested in 2012 for "hooliganism" in what country?

112. What band performed cancelled tour dates so they could play their hit "Everlong" on the David Letterman show on his first show back from heart surgery in 2000?

Answers

106) Twenty One Pilots
108) Black Eyed Peas
110) "All I Want For Christmas is You"
112) Foo Fighters

107) One Direction
109) Torey Lanez
111) Russia*

*The band had staged several protest concerts protesting Vladimir Putin, and the Orthodox Church of Russia for their support of him. Two of the band members served 21 months in a Russian prison, garnering international attention and protest.

113. Who had their first top ten single in 2005 with "Beverly Hills"?

114. Whose 2001 album "Yankee Hotel Foxtrot" was rated the third best album of the decade by Rolling Stone Magazine?

115. Who had their highest charting single ever in 2003 when he released his duet with Sheryl Crow, "Picture"?

116. What boy band reunited after a six-year hiatus in 2019 to release the single "Sucker," which debuted at number one on the Billboard chart?

117. What rapper was shot and killed on March 31, 2019, outside of a store he owned named The Marathon?

118. Doja Cat and Nicki Manaj became the first female rap duo to top the Billboard Hot 200 in 2020 with what song?

119. What country music star signed a contract to play for the New York Mets in spring training of 2000?

Answers

113) Weezer

114) Wilco

115) Kid Rock

116) Jonas Brothers

117) Nipsey Hussle

118) "Say So"

119) Garth Brooks*

*Brooks, who went to Oklahoma State University on scholarship to throw the javelin, tried out in spring training for three different major league teams. The San Diego Padres in 1998 and 1999, the New York Mets in 2000, and the Kansas City Royals in 2004.

120. What musician married the lead singer of Nickelback, Chad Kroeger, in 2012 after one month of dating?

121. In the year 2002, the most played song on Canadian radio was "The Middle" by what band?

122. What band did Spencer Elden sue in 2021 because they used a picture of him naked as a baby grasping for a dollar bill on their album cover 30 years earlier?

123. What Billie Eilish song spent 19 weeks at number one in 2019?

124. What band performed the theme song for the hit comedy series "Big Bang Theory" which premiered in 2007?

125. What 2009 hit by Miley Cyrus begins with "I hopped off the plane at LAX with a dream and my cardigan"?

126. What actress played June Carter Cash in the 2005 movie "Walk the Line"?

Answers

120) Avril Lavigne
122) Nirvana*
124) Barenaked Ladies
126) Reece Witherspoon

121) Jimmy Eat World
123) "Bad Guy"
125) "Party in the U.S.A."

*Elden claimed the iconic picture on the cover of the band's "Nevermind" album was child pornography. A Judge dismissed the case in early 2022 before it ever got to trial.

127. Name the American country music supergroup formed in 2019 featuring Amanda Shires, Natalie Hemby, Maren Morris, and Brandi Carlile.

128. Gavin Degraw had a top ten hit in 2005 with the song "I Don't Want to Be." What popular teen drama was it the theme song to?

129. What rapper posed as Jesus on the cover of Rolling Stone Magazine in 2006?

130. Whose 2008 album "Paper Trail" included the number one hits "Live Your Life" and "Whatever You Like"?

131. What British singer married supermodel Heidi Klum in 2005?

132. Whose second album "21" was the best-selling album of 2011?

133. Who had his third number one country song in 2002 with "I'm Gonna Miss Her (The Fishin' Song)"?

Answers

127) The Highwomen
129) Kanye West
131) Seal
133) Brad Paisley

128) "One Tree Hill"
130) T.I.
132) Adele*

*"21" was the second album ever to sell a million digital copies. The first was Eminem's "Recovery."

134. In what 2002 film did Britney Spears star as a character named Lucy Wagner?

135. Name the Australian born singer whose 21st century hits include "Saturday Sun," "Mess is Mine," and "Riptide."

136. Name the singer whose residency at Caesar's Palace in Las Vegas "New Day" ran from 2003 to 2007 and is the highest grossing residency in the history of Las Vegas.

137. What country music singer married actor Eddie Cibrian in 2011?

138. Who won the Grammy for both "Song of the Year" and "Best Pop Solo Performance" for his 2014 hit, "Thinking Out Loud"?

139. Who had back-to-back number one hits in 2004 with "Yeah!" and "Burn"?

140. What 2014 movie soundtrack reached number one on the Billboard 200 albums chart, becoming the first movie soundtrack in history to reach the top spot while comprised completely of previously released songs?

Answers

134) "Crossroads" 135) Vance Joy
136) Celine Dion 137) LeAnn Rimes*
138) Ed Sheeran 139) Usher
140) "Guardians of the Galaxy"

*Rimes and Cibrian met on the set of the movie "Northern Lights" and began having an affair while both married. Cibrian was married to "Desperate Housewives" star Brandi Glanville.

141. Name the hard rock band whose "Not in This Lifetime Tour," which began in 2016 is one of the five highest grossing tours of all time?

142. Name the singer who appeared on "Sesame Street" in 2010, but later had her part edited out after viewers complained that her dress was too revealing for a children's show?

143. Name the female country music singer who became the first artist in history to have six straight number one country albums after her "Storyteller" reached the top of the chart in 2016.

144. Who had a top three hit in 2000 with "Thong Song"?

145. Who had a number one album in 2010 with "Animal" and another in 2017 with "Rainbow"?

146. Who, in 2019 became the first solo artist to ever hold the top three spots on the Billboard chart at the same time?

147. Who won five Grammy awards in 2003, including best song for "Don't Know Why"?

Answers

141) Guns N' Roses

142) Katy Perry

143) Carrie Underwood

144) Sisqo

145) Kesha

146) Ariana Grande

147) Norah Jones*

Jones is the daughter of Indian sitarist and producer Ravi Shankar.

148. What 60-year-old singer's "Twenty-Four Seven" tour was the top grossing tour of the year 2000?

149. Who, in 2003, became the first ever rapper to win an Oscar for Best Original Song?

150. Whose "No Shoes, No Shirt, No Problems" album, released in 2002, included five top ten country singles?

151. What band won seven Grammy awards for their 2006 album "Taking the Long Way"?

152. What female recording artist proposed to her boyfriend Carey Hart in 2005, while he was competing in a motocross race?

153. Name the English band whose hits include "Dog Days Are Over," "Shake It Out," and "Cosmic Love."

154. What superstar had her first major acting role as Foxxy Cleopatra in the 2002 movie "Austin Powers in Goldmember"?

Answers

148) Tina Turner

149) Eminem

150) Kenny Chesney

151) The Chicks

152) Pink*

153) Florence and the Machine

154) Beyonce

*At the Pro 250 class finals, Pink held up a sign that said, "Will you marry me?" Hart didn't stop. On the next lap, Pink held up a sign which read "I'm serious!" Hart then pulled over and said yes.

155. What singer and actress rose to national fame by playing the character Mitchie Torres in the musical television film "Camp Rock" in 2008?

156. Name the band which includes twin brothers Joel and Benji Madden, which achieved breakthrough success with their second album "The Young and the Hopeless" in 2002.

157. In 2019, a sweater worn by what deceased artist when his band filmed their 1992 MTV Unplugged sold for $334,000?

158. Jessica Simpson married Nick Lachey in 2002. What boy band was Lachey a member of at the time?

159. On what Fox network comedy drama series about a Boston lawyer did Elton John make a guest appearance in 2001?

160. Who became the first male artist in nearly a decade to have his debut single top the chart with his 2005 song "Run It"?

161. Whose "Double Live" album became the first live album to sell 20 million copies in America in 2006, eight years after it was released?

Answers

155) Demi Lovato

156) Good Charlotte

157) Kurt Cobain*

158) 98 Degrees

1589) "Ally McBeal"

160) Chris Brown

161) Garth Brooks

Cobain's widow Courtney Love gifted the sweater to Jackie Farry, her friend and nanny to Kurt and Courtney's daughter Frances Bean. After battling cancer for ten years, Farry had to sell the sweater to help pay for her medical expenses.

162. Name the virtual band whose hits include "Clint Eastwood," "Feel Good Inc.," and "On Melancholy Hill."

163. Whose third album "24K Magic," released in 2016, won seven Grammy awards?

164. Whose debut album "Country Grammar" containing the hit "Ride Wit Me" went on to sell over ten million copies?

165. In the 2007 "Simpsons" movie, what band is sunk into Lake Springfield early in the movie?

166. Who, in 2022 played a few notes on a flute that was once owned by President James Madison?

167. Who won both an Oscar and Golden Globe award for his song "Glory" from the 2015 movie "Selma"?

168. Nicknamed "The Queen of rap," who did Billboard Magazine say was the best-selling female rap artist of the 2010s?

Answers

162) Gorillaz
164) Nelly
166) Lizzo
168) Nicki Minaj*

163) Bruno Mars
165) Green Day
167) John Legend

Some sources list Minaj as the best-selling female rap artist of all time, while others say the honor belongs to Missy Elliot.

169. What female artist had their second number one hit in 2022 with "About Damn Time"?

170. What female country singer won the Grammy for Album of the Year for her 2019 release "Golden Hour"?

171. The band O.A.R. has had hits in the 21st century including "Love and Memories" and "Shattered (Turn the Car Around.)". What does O.A.R. stand for?

172. What band had their fifth number one country hit in 2016 with "H.O.L.Y."?

173. What American band's debut studio album "Is This It" is considered by critics to be one of the best albums of 2001?

174. All members of what hard rock band signed a "cessation of touring" agreement in 2014, swearing they would never tour together again?

175. Who had a number one hit for six weeks in 2009 with "Right Round"?

Answers

169) Lizzo

170) Kacey Musgraves

171) "Of a Revolution"

172) Florida Georgia Line

173) The Strokes

174) Motley Crue*

175) Flo Rida

*In 2021 they blew up the agreement and toured again citing "a whole new generation of Crueheads are demanding the band get back together.

176. The Eagles played their last concert with what band member on July 29, 2015?

177. What superstar named her first baby "Axl" in 2013, after having a dream about watching Guns and Roses front man Axl Rose perform in her dream?

178. Who won the MTV Video Music award for best video in 2004 for "Hey Ya!"?

179. In 2013, ten million people tuned into the final episode of a television show, which ended by playing "Baby Blue" by Badfinger. What was the name of the show?

180. Who had a hit in 2003 singing about "Stacy's Mom"?

181. Who had their ninth and final, as of 2023, number one hit in the U.K. in 2000 with "Holler/Let Love Lead the Way"?

182. What female musical star's father, Atz Kilcher, stars in the Discovery channel's reality series 'Alaska: The Last Frontier"?

Answers

176) Glen Frey
177) Fergie
178) Outkast
179) "Breaking Bad"*
180) Fountains of Wayne
181) Spice Girls
182) Jewel

*The song was chosen to represent lead character Walter White's skills and cooking high quality meth. He is near death, and the song starts with the lyric "Guess I got what I deserve."

183. What legendary rap group was the 2015 biopic "Straight Outta Compton" about?

184. After Rage Against the Machine broke up in 2000, three members joined former Soundgarden front man Chris Cornell to form what band?

185. What singer released her debut album "When We All Fall Asleep, Where Do We Go?" at the age of seventeen in 2019, which debuted at number one in the United States?

186. Who won the Grammy for Best Rock Album for his 2002 release "The Rising"?

187. What rock legend released a 16-minute song about the assassination of John F. Kennedy titled "Murder Most Foul" in 2020?

188. What hip hop star sold his clothing company "Rocawear" for $204 million in 2007?

189. What country music legend died by suicide on April 30, 2022, one day before she was to be inducted into the Country Music Hall of Fame?

Answers

183) N.W.A.

184) Audioslave

185) Billie Eilish

186) Bruce Springsteen

187) Bob Dylan*

188) Jay-Z

189) Naomi Judd

Although the song is primarily about the murder of JFK, it is also filled with references about American culture in the 1960s.

190. As of January 2023, what single by the Weeknd is the most streamed song in the history of Spotify?

191. What country is the duo Daft Punk from?

192. Whose "Summertime Sadness" went to Number six on the chart in 2013, the highest on the chart of any song in her career?

193. The rapper Takeoff was shot and killed outside of a bowling alley in Houston in 2022. What group was a member of?

194. In 2002, what future star was the first winner of the television show "American Idol"?

195. What 22-year-old female singer died in a plane crash in the Bahamas on August 25, 2001?

196. Whose 2009 album "Feel That Fire" included two songs which reached number one on the country chart: The title track, and "Sideway"?

Answers

190) "Blinding Lights" *   191) France
192) Lana Del Rey   193) Migos
194) Kelly Clarkson   195) Aaliyah
196) Dierks Bentley

*"Blinding Lights" surpassed Ed Sheeran's "Shape of You" in early January 2023. As of early 2023, "Dance Monkey" by Tones and I is in third, "Someone You Loved" by Lewis Capaldi is fourth.

197. What music superstar was pronounced dead at the U.C.L.A. medical center on June 25, 2009?

198. What group was dropped from radio station playlists after their lead singer said on stage in London in 2003, "Just so you know, we are ashamed that the President of the United States is from Texas"?

199. The deadliest mass shooting in American history occurred on October 1, 2017, at the Route 91 Harvest Festival in which city?

200. What star of movies and television did Kid Rock marry in 2006?

201. What artist famously had one of her breasts exposed when Justin Timberlake ripped off a portion of her costume during their halftime performance at the 2004 Super Bowl?

202. Whose album "Shoot for the Stars, Aim for the Moon" debuted at number one on July 3, 2020, less than five months after he was murdered in Los Angeles?

203. Whose fourteenth studio album "Mandatory Fun" became his first ever to top the chart in 2014?

Answers

197) Michael Jackson
198) The Chicks*
199) Las Vegas
200) Pamela Anderson
201) Janet Jackson
202) Pop Smoke
203) Weird Al Yankovic

*The Chicks were blacklisted by over 1000 radio stations across the United States because of the comment. President Bush, however, defended their right to criticize him saying, "That's one of the great things about America."

204. Who had their most successful single to date in 2002 with 'Work It"?

205. Who became the first female artist to have four albums debut at number one in 2003?

206. Who had a number one hit in 2001 in the United States with "It Wasn't Me"?

207. In 2017, whose album "For All the Right Reasons" became only the fourth by a Canadian artist to sell ten million copies?

208. Name the band whose most successful single "Fat Lip" appeared on its 2001 debut album titled "All Killer No Filler"?

209. Who launched her "Material Girl" line of clothing in 2010, with the help of her 13-year-old daughter Lourdes?

210. What is the title of the 2003 movie in which Jack Black poses as a substitute teacher who forms a band with the students?

Answers

204) Missy Elliot
206) Shaggy
208) Sum 41
210) "School of Rock"

205) Britney Spears
207) Nickleback
209) Madonna

*Shaggy says the song was inspired by the Eddie Murphy comedy special "Raw" in which Murphy instructs the audience to deny everything even if caught red handed.

211. Who, in 2017 became the youngest person to receive the Kennedy Center Honors, and the first rapper to do so?

212. Who became the first artist to have a number one hit in four different decades when her Christmas song topped the chart for a third straight week in January, 2020?

213. What rock legend performed one his most famous songs at halftime of the 2007 Super Bowl, ironically, while it rained?

214. What superstar voiced the character "Gazelle" in the 2016 Disney animated movie "Zootopia"?

215. Name the lead singer of the band Matchbox 20 who released his first solo album titled "Something to Be" in 2005.

216. Who created a dance sensation with their 2015 release "Watch Me (Whip/Nae Nae)"?

217. Rascal Flatts reached the top ten of the U.S. pop charts with their cover of Tom Cochrane's "Life is a Highway." What Pixar film featured it on the soundtrack in 2006?

Answers

211) LL Cool J

212) Mariah Carey

213) Prince

214) Shakira

215) Rob Thomas

216) Silento*

217) "Cars"

*"Watch Me (Whip/Nae Nae)" was the biggest dance sensation of 2015. The Nae Nae was based on the character Sheneneh, played by Martin Lawrence in the 1990s Television series, "Martin."

218. In 2015, who had 14 songs in the Hot 100, after the release of his mixtape "If You're Reading This It's Too Late?

219. What popular artist dropped the dollar sign from the spelling of her name in 2014?

220. What band's 2007- 2008 reunion tour of 151 shows was the third highest grossing tour of all time (at the time).

221. Whose third album titled "8701," released in 2001, contained the number one hits "U Remind Me" and "U Got It Bad"?

222. What Lizzo song went to number one in 2019, nearly two years after it was released, after appearing in the Netflix movie titled "Someone Great"?

223. What rapper died of an accidental overdose on September 7, 2018, at the age of 26?

224. What is the name of the 2001 movie starring Mark Wahlberg as the lead singer of a tribute band who ends up joining his favorite group?

Answers

218) Drake

219) Kesha

220) The Police

221) Usher

222) "Truth Hurts"

223) Mac Miller

224) "Rock Star"

The Police reunion tour has since dropped to number 17 on the list of the highest grossing tours of all time.

225. Whose 2021 hit "Driver's License" stayed at number one for eight weeks?

226. What is the popular music duo comprised of Tyler Joseph and Josh Dun better known as?

227. Who won the Grammy Award for Best New Artist in 2015, and the Grammy for Record of the Year for "Stay with Me"?

228. What is the name of the bassist for the band Fall Out Boy who was married to Ashlee Simpson from 2008 to 2011?

229. What rock legend teamed with Alison Krauss to with the 2009 Grammy for Album of the Year with "Raising Sand"?

230. Justin Timberlake's 2004 hit "Cry Me A River" was inspired by his breakup with what musical superstar?

231. What future superstar released her debut album, which was gospel, in 2001 at the age of 16 under her real name, Katy Hudson?

Answers

225) Olivia Rodrigo
226) Twenty One Pilots*
227) Sam Smith
228) Pete Wentz
229) Robert Plant
230) Britney Spears
231) Katy Perry

The name "Twenty One Pilots was inspired by an Arthur Miller play titled "All My Sons." The play is about a man who commits suicide after selling faulty parts for airplanes, causing the death of 21 pilots in World War Two.

232. Name the daughter of a music superstar who was once married to a music superstar who died on January 12, 2023.

233. What now famous catch phrase first appeared in a Saturday Night Live skit in the year 2000 in which featured Christopher Walken and Will Ferrell?

234. For what punk rock band does Laura Jane Grace, who was born as Thomas Gabel until gender reassignment surgery, serve as the lead singer and songwriter?

235. What band's second album titled "Three Cheers for Sweet Revenge," released in 2004, included the hits "Helena" and "I'm Not Okay (I Promise)"?

236. In 2016, three members who were part of what highly popular band formed a new band called GEM?

237. What popular television series featuring competing singers debuted on June 11, 2002?

238. At precisely midnight on January 1, 2000, Prince played what song for what he said would be the final time?

Answers

232) Lisa Marie Presley
234) Against Me!
236) Spice Girls
238) "1999"*

233) "More Cowbell"
235) My Chemical Romance
237) "American Idol"

*Prince brought the song back in 2007 during his halftime performance at the Super Bowl, and it appeared often in his set lists after.

239. Jeon Jung-Kook was ranked by Rolling Stone Magazine as the 191st greatest singer of all time. For what highly popular band does he serve as a vocalist?

240. What soundtrack was the best-selling album of 2006?

241. Who became the first person in history to hold the top three spots on the British Singles chart in 2016 with "Love Yourself," "Sorry," and "Believe"?

242. For what successful band has Adam Levine served as lead singer since 2001?

243. Whose album "Fearless" won both the Grammy for Album of the Year, and the C.M.A. for best Country Music Album in 2009?

244. Who became the first artist to have ten consecutive albums debut at number one on the Billboard 200 album chart with his 2020 release titled "Music to Be Murdered By"?

245. Who had their only number one single in 2001 with "Family Affair"?

Answers

239) BTS

240) "High School Musical"

241) Justin Bieber

242) Maroon Five*

243) Taylor Swift

244) Eminem

245) Mary J. Blige

*Levine, also a coach on "The Voice," was named People Magazine's "Sexiest Man Alive" in 2019.

246. What is the singer and songwriter who was born Solana Imani Rowe better known as?

247. What band's song "Cruise" set a record for most consecutive weeks on top of the hot country chart with 22 in 2013?

248. What 2011 hit by Adele begins with "She, she ain't real. She ain't gon' be able to love you like I will. She is a stranger. You and I have history"?

249. In 2019 and 2020, the event known as EDC was nominated for music festival of the year. What does EDC stand for?

250. What 2001 film starring Denzel Washington featured cameo appearances by both Snoop Dogg and Dr. Dre?

251. Who released their eighth studio album, titled "Endless Summer Vacation" on March 10, 2023?

252. What band had number one hits in 2008 with "Use Somebody" and "Sex on Fire"?

Answers

246) SZA
248) "Rumor Has It"
250) "Training Day"
252) Kings of Leon

247) Florida Georgia Line*
249) Electric Daisy Carnival
251) Miley Cyrus

*"Cruise" was surpassed in 2017 when Sam Hunt's "Body Like a Back Road" stayed at number one for 24 weeks.

253. What rapper had their first number one single in 2011 with "Give Me Everything"?

254. What singer became the first female to have 400 million Instagram followers in 2023?

255. What was the title of the 2018 single from the "A Star is Born" soundtrack by Lady Gaga and Bradley Cooper which went to number one in over 30 countries?

256. Who won the Grammy for Best Country Song for his 2004 release "Live Like You Were Dying"?

257. What rapper had his highest charting single in 2018 when he teamed with Drake on "Going Bad"?

258. What band's album "Songs of Innocence" was automatically downloaded to anyone with an active iTunes account in 2014?

259. What band's 2001 titled "Iowa" is considered to be one of the best heavy metal albums of the 21st century?

Answers

253) Pitbull

254) Selena Gomez

255) "Shallow"

256) Tim McGraw*

257) Meek Mill

258) U2

259) Slipknot

*Although McGraw did not write the song, it struck a chord with him because his own father was dying the first time he read the lyrics. His father, former Major League Baseball pitcher Tim McGraw, died two weeks before Tim McGraw recorded the song.

260. John Entwistle died in a Las Vegas Hotel in 2002 at the age of 57. For what legendary band did he serve as the bass player?

261. Name the 2009 hit by Train which includes the lines "Your lipstick stains on the front lobe of my left side brains. I knew I wouldn't forget you, and so I went and let you blow my mind"

262. Name the Canadian singer who had her only top 40 hit in the U.S. with her 2007 single "1234."

263. What rapper was featured on Dua Lipa's smash hit "Levitating" in 2020?

264. What controversial hip hop superstar visited President Donald Trump at the White House on October 11, 2018?

265. Who won the Grammy for "Best Country Album" for her 2019 release "Wildcard"?

266. Troy Gentry died in a helicopter crash in New Jersey in 2017. What highly successful country music duo was he a part of?

Answers

260) The Who   * 261) "Hey Soul Sister"
262) Feist   263) DaBaby
264) Kanye West   265) Miranda Lambert
266) Montgomery Gentry

*In 2011, Rolling Stone Magazine readers voted Entwistle "The Greatest Bass Player of All Time."

267. Who became the first solo female in history to win the Grammy for Best Rap Album as a solo artist in 2019 with "Invasion of Privacy"?

268. Gwen Stefani makes a cameo on the arm of Leonardo DiCaprio in what 2004 film?

269. What is the title of the 2006 song by Daniel Powter that was the best-selling single in the United States in 2006?

270. What female Superstar performed the National Anthem prior to the Super Bowl in 2004 when it was played in her hometown of Houston?

271. What Nine Inch Nails song did Johnny Cash release a cover of to commercial and critical success in 2002?

272. What singer, nicknamed the "Queen of Soul," died August 16, 2018?

273. Who won her first Grammy in 2005 for her song "Toxic" which won for "Best Dance Recording"?

Answers

267) Cardi B*

268) "The Aviator"

269) "Bad Day"

270) Beyonce

271) "Hurt"

272) Aretha Franklin

273) Britney Spears

Both Rolling Stone and Pitchfork magazines listed "Invasion of Privacy" as the best album of 2019.

274. In 2022, Harry Styles set a record for a song that spent the most weeks in the top two positions on Billboard's Hot 100. What song of his spent 25 weeks either at number one or number two?

275. What rap star is the owner and C.E.O. of the label "Young Money Entertainment"?

276. What male country star had his tenth county number one hit in 2007 with "Letter to Me"?

277. In 2001. which female superstar signed what was, at the time, the largest contract in music history, a six-album deal with Arista Records for over $100 million.

278. Name the artist whose "Farewell Yellow Brick Road" is the highest grossing tour of all time (as of June 2023)?

279. Who won Grammys for Best Rap Song and Best Rap Performance in 2015 for his song "I"?

280. Name the artist who wrote the song "Royals" at the age of 13, which would sell over ten million copies and win the Grammy for Song of the Year in 2014.

Answers

274) "As it Was"   275) Lil Wayne
276) Brad Paisley   277) Whitney Houston
278) Elton John   279) Kendrick Lamar
280) Lorde*

Lorde wrote the song in thirty minutes, while on lunch at school. She got the inspiration for the title by seeing a picture of Kansas City Royals Baseball Hall of Famer George Brett.

281. What female singing superstar starred in a semi-autobiographical film titled "Glitter" in 2001?

282. Whose "Never Say Never," released in 2011, became the highest grossing concert film of all time?

283. What country band capped an impressive comeback by winning five Grammys at the 2007 show, including Best Album for "Taking the Long Way"?

284. Who had a number one hit in 2006 with "You're Beautiful"?

285. What boy band had two of the top five selling albums in the United States in 2012, including their debut album "Up All Night"?

286. In what city would you find MoPop, or the Museum of Pop Culture, which opened in the year 2000 as the Experience Music Project?

287. What was the title of the 2018 feature film about the life of rock icon Freddie Mercury?

Answers

281) Mariah Carey
283) The Chicks
285) One Direction
287) "Bohemian Rhapsody"

282) Justin Bieber
284) James Blunt*
286) Seattle

The song is often thought of as sweetly romantic, but Blunt wrote it about a man on drugs who is stalking someone else's girlfriend.

288. Whose fifth album "Tickets to My Downfall" was the only album of 2020 to debut at number one on the Billboard 200 Album chart?

289. What legendary rock band performed in front of over a half million fans in Cuba in 2016, the first time the country had hosted a major concert since 1959?

290. Whose second album "Contra" went to number one on the Billboard 200 in the year 2010?

291. Who performed at halftime of the Super Bowl in 2023, later revealing that she did so while pregnant with her second child?

292. What rapper referenced having a sexual relationship with Taylor Swift in his 2016 song "Famous"?

293. Who, in 2022, became the youngest woman ever to have won an Emmy, Grammy, Oscar, and Tony, and only the second African American woman to do so?

294. Who won three consecutive Grammy Awards for Best Country Duo/Group Performance from 2019 to 2021?

Answers

288) Machine Gun Kelly

289) The Rolling Stones

290) Vampire Weekend

291) Rihanna

292) Kanye West*

293) Jennifer Hudson

294) Dan and Shay

*West and Swift have had on and off again feud which began in 2009 when West interrupted Swift's acceptance speech at the MTV Video Music Awards contesting that Beyonce should have won the award.

295. What country music superstar first rose to national prominence by winning the fourth season of "American Idol" in 2005?

296. What Saturday Night Live cast member did Ariana Grande meet, and later become engaged to, when she hosted the show in 2016?

297. Country music's Vince Gill married what other musical superstar in the year 2000?

298. What band went on the "Joshua Tree" tour in 2017 to celebrate the 30th anniversary of them releasing an album of the same name?

299. What band set the record for most Grammy wins for "Best Rock Album" in 2022, with their album "Medicine at Midnight"?

300. What band became the first non-English speaking group to sell out a concert at the Rose Bowl in 2019?

301. Whose 2011 song "Born This Way" reached number one in over 25 million countries?

Answers

295) Carrie Underwood

296) Pete Davidson

297) Amy Grant

298) U2

299) Foo Fighters

300) BTS

301) Lady Gaga*

"The song was inspired by the gay disco anthem "I Was Born This Way" by Carl Bean in 1977.

302. What rapper's album "My Turn" spent five weeks on top of the Billboard 200 in 2020?

303. Name the country music duo formed by Jennifer Nettles and Kristian Bush whose debut single "Baby Girl" went to number two on the Billboard Hot Country Chart in 2003.

304. What legendary trumpet player and vocalist was the airport in New Orleans renamed after in 2001?

305. Who reached number six on the U.S. Billboard Chart in 2017 with "Sorry Not Sorry"?

306. Pink, Christina Aguilera, Lil' Kim, and Mya had a number one hit in 2001 with their cover of "Lady Marmalade" from what movie soundtrack?

307. What 2013 song by Daft Punk, featuring Pharrell Williams, went on to win the Grammy for Record of the Year and Best Performance by a Duo or Group?

308. What famous family band is comprised of siblings Nick, Kevin, and Joe?

Answers

302) Lil Baby

303) Sugarland

304) Louis Armstrong

305) Demi Lovato*

306) "Moulin Rouge"

307) "Get Lucky"

308) Jonas Brothers

*Lovato was born in Dallas, Texas, where her mother was a country music recording artist as well as a Dallas Cowboy Cheerleader.

309. What band's second album "Cleopatra," released in 2016 featured the single "Ophelia" which would be the most played song on alternative radio in that year?

310. In 2010 a supergroup known as "Artists for Haiti" recorded a remake of what 1985 song to raise money for victims of a 7.0 earthquake in Haiti earlier that year?

311. In August 2019, who became the first artist born in the 21st century to have a number one hit on the Billboard Hot 100?

312. What rapper, who was the first artist to have five consecutive albums debut at number one, died at the age of 50 on April 9, 2021?

313. What rock legend married former model Heather Mills on June 11, 2002?

314. Whose 2014 video for her song "Anaconda" would go on to be the first video of a solo female rap song to reach one billion views on YouTube?

315. Based largely on the strength of his album "Noel," who was the top selling musician of the year 2007?

Answers

309) The Lumineers

310) "We Are the World"

311) Billie Eilish

312) DMX

313) Paul McCartney

314) Nicki Minaj*

315) Josh Groban

*Released on August 19, 2014, the video was viewed 19.6 million times in the first day, setting the record for most views by a YouTube video in a 24 hour time frame.

316. Who won her 28ᵗʰ Grammy in 2021, giving her the most of those trophies of any female in history?

317. Who became the first rapper to hold a top spot on the New York Times bestseller list when his novel "Supermarket" topped the Paperback Trade Fiction list?

318. Name the popular electronic and DJ production duo comprised of Alexander Pall and Andrew Taggart.

319. What Rock and Roll Hall of Fame member had their fifth number one album in 2005 with "Devils and Dust"?

320. What actress did Coldplay lead vocalist Chris Martin marry on December 5, 2003?

321. The television series "Moesha" aired its final episode on May 14, 2001. What pop star and model played the role of Moesha?

322. In 2012, Drake and Chris Brown got into a fight at a New York City night club. The fight was reportedly over what music star who they both had dated?

Answers

316) Beyonce

317) Logic

318) The Chainsmokers

319) Bruce Springsteen

320) Gwyneth Paltrow

321) Brandy

322) Rihanna*

*The feud between Drake and Brown continued for several years, but they buried the hatchet and worked together on the song "No Guidance" which won three Soul Train Music awards and went to number five on the Billboard Hot 100.

323. What boy band reunited in 2019 to have their first number one album in nearly 20 years, titled "DNA"?

324. Who, in 2003 at the age of 21, became the youngest singer ever to have a star placed on the Hollywood Walk of Fame?

325. Name the artist, ranked 26th on VH1's list of the top 100 female singers of all time, whose song "Love is a Losing Game" was named by George Michael as his favorite all time song.

326. What pop star released her first country album in 2008 titled "Do You Know" which peaked at number one on the country chart and number four on the Billboard 200 chart?

327. What British band led by Matty Healy went to number one with their second album "I Like It When You Sleep, for You Are So Beautiful Yet So Unaware of It"?

328. What iconic star joined with Lady Gaga to make two albums in the 21st century: "Cheek to Cheek" and "Love for Sale"?

329. Whose 2013 album "Crash My Party" was named Album of the Decade by the Academy of Country Music?

Answers

323) Backstreet Boys
325) Amy Winehouse
327) The 1975
329) Luke Bryan

324) Britney Spears
326) Jessica Simpson
328) Tony Bennett*

Bennett set the record for oldest artist ever to release an album of new material with "Love for Sale" in 2021 at the age of 95 years and 60 days.

330. Name the singer, songwriter, and actor who starred as Jesus, and produced the NBC remake of "Jesus Christ Superstar" in 2018, which he won an Emmy for.

331. What country does the band Arcade Fire hail from?

332. What is the rapper, singer-songwriter, and producer born with the name Tyler Gregory Okonma better known as?

333. Who, in 2014 with the release of her album "Partners" became the first artist to have number one albums in six consecutive decades?

334. What Portland, Oregon based band had a number one hit on the Billboard Modern Rock chart in 2004 with "Float On"?

335. What rapper plays the role of Tej Parker in the "Fast and Furious" movie series?

336. What country legend had his 41st number one hit in 2004 with "Give it Away" breaking Conway Twitty's record for most number one country hits?

Answers

330) John Legend

331) Canada

332) Tyler, the Creator

333) Barbra Streisand

334) Modest Mouse

335) Ludacris*

336) George Strait

*Ludacris is distant cousins with comedian and movie star Richard Pryor, as well as the pop star known as Monica.

337. Who paired with Jay -Z to have the last number one hit of 2009 with "Empire State of Mind"?

338. What pop superstar met actor Liam Hemsworth while filming the movie "The Last Song," whom she would later marry?

339. Whose "Crazy" was named the best song of 2006 by Rolling Stone Magazine?

340. What legendary jam band led by Trey Anastasio reunited in 2008 after a brief break up, continuing to be one of America's most popular jam bands?

341. In 2020, who became the youngest male artist ever to have released four studio albums which reached number one on the Billboard 200 chart?

342. Name the Australian artist whose single "Can't Get You Out of My Head" reached number one in 40 countries and was the biggest selling hit of her career?

343. Who won a Grammy for "Best Country Song" for his 2017 release "Broken Halos"?

Answers

337) Alicia Keys
339) Gnarls Barkley*
341) Shawn Mendes
343) Chris Stapleton

338) Miley Cyrus
340) Phish
342) Kylie Minogue

*The name "Gnarls Barkley" is a play on hall of fame basketball star and television commentator Charles Barkley.

344. In 2013, a concert film titled "This is Us" was released and went on to gross nearly $70 million. Which band was it about?

345. What pop superstar made a cameo appearance as a member of the Lannister army in the seventh season of the blockbuster HBO series "Game of Thrones"?

346. Name the show which debuted in 2003 on CMT which pairs country musicians to perform with artists from other genres.

347. The film "Rocketman" premiered on May 16, 2017. What rock legend is the main subject of the film?

348. What is the title of the song by Gotye featuring Kimbra was the best-selling song of 2012?

349. According to Forbes Magazine, in 2017 who was the first rapper to become a billionaire?

350. What duo had two number one singles in 2013, "Thrift Shop" and "Can't Hold Us"?

Answers

344) One Direction

345) Ed Sheeran

346) "Crossroads"*

347) Elton John

348) "Somebody That I Used To Know"

349) Jay-Z

350) Macklemore and Ryan Lewis

The first paring was of Elvis Costello and Lucinda Williams.

351. What rock legend played Captain Edward Teague in the 2007 film "Pirates of the Caribbean: At World's End"?

352. Whose fifth album to be released after his death "Loyal to the Game" went to number one in 2005?

353. What artist posted a picture of her pregnant with twins on Instagram on February 1, 2017, which was liked eight million times in the first 24 hours?

354. What country music singer had a number one album in 2014 with his fourth release, "Outsiders"?

355. Who had their first mainstream hit single with their 2012 release "Summertime Sadness"?

356. The soundtrack to the 2010 film "Iron Man 2" consisted entirely of songs by what legendary hard rock band?

357. What band was nominated for the Grammy for "Song of the Year" in 2013 for "How You Remind Me"?

Answers

351) Keith Richards

352) Tupac Shakur*

353) Beyonce

354) Eric Church

355) Lana Del Rey

356) AC/DC

357) Nickleback

*Tupac is tied with Notorious B.I.G. for having the most posthumous number one albums, as each have three.

358. Who appeared on the cover of Rolling Stone Magazine for the 23rd time in 2021, the most such appearances by a female artist in the history of the magazine?

359. At 10 minutes, 13 seconds, what Taylor Swift song became the longest to reach the top spot on the pop chart in 2021?

360. What city in Tennessee declared January 8, 2010, "Elvis Presley Day" on what have been the King's 75th birthday, in part because he had a famous residence there?

361. Name the star who was born on October 28, 1987, in Long Beach, California with the name Christopher Edwin Breaux.

362. What rapper joined Jennifer Lopez on the 2003 hit "All I Have" which topped the Billboard Hot 100 for four consecutive weeks?

363. Born Jason Bradley Deford, what is the name of the singer and rapper who won three CMT Music Awards for "Son of a Sinner" in 2023 better known as?

364. Name the artist whose version of "I Dreamed a Dream" became the fastest selling single in the history of the United Kingdom after she performed it on "Britain's Got Talent" in 2009.

Answers

358) Madonna

359) "All Too Well (Taylor's Version)"*

360) Memphis, Tennessee

361) Frank Ocean

362) L.L. Cool J

363) Jelly Roll

364) Susan Boyle

*"All Too Well" broke the record for longest number one song previously held by Don McClean's "American Pie.

365. Legendary entertainers David Bowie, George Michael, Prince, Glen Frey, and Merle Haggard all died the same year. What year was that?

366. What Pink Floyd album made a surprise return to the charts in 2013 when it was discounted to 99 cents in the Google Play store?

367. A song about what city gave George Ezra have his first hit in 2014?

368. Whose debut release "College Dropout" won the Grammy for Best Rap Album in 2005?

369. Who, in 2001, became the first artist to have both the number one album and the number one movie in America at the same time?

370. Name the female artist, who rose to fame on Myspace, whose 2007 debut album "Coco" included the hit singles "Bubbly" and "Realize."

371. What heavy metal band had their fifth consecutive number one album in 2015 with "Immortalized"?

Answers

365) 2016

367) Budapest

369) Jennifer Lopez*

371) Disturbed

366) "Dark Side of the Moon"

368) Kanye West

370) Colbie Caillat

*The movie was "The Wedding Planner," and the album was titled "J. Lo."

372. What band. led by Gwen Stefani, had a hit single in 2002 with "Hella Good"?

373. Who, in 2020, became the first artist to have a number one album in the U.S. to be recorded in entirely in a non-English language?

374. What pop music superstar was actor Nick Cannon married to from 2008 to 2016?

375. The video for what song became the first to reach 10 billion views on YouTube in 2022?

376. Rock legend David Crosby made headlines in the year 2000 by revealing he was the surrogate father for two children of what singer?

377. Who had her fourth number one country single in 2007 with the release of "So Small" from the album "Carnival Ride"?

378. When her single "You Haven't Seen the Last of Me" went to number one on the U.S. dance chart in 2011, who became the first artist have a number one song on a billboard chart in six consecutive decades?

Answers

372) No Doubt

373) Bad Bunny

374) Mariah Carey

375) "Baby Shark"

376) Melissa Ethridge*

377) Carrie Underwood

378) Cher

One of the two children that Crosby fathered for Ethridge and her partner, Julie Cypher, passed away due to causes related to opioid addiction in 2020 at the age of 21.

379. What was the name of the number one hit in 2015 by Wiz Khalifa featuring Charlie Puth, released as a tribute to actor Paul Walker?

380. In January of 2018 Dolores O'Riordan died in London at the age of 46. What band was she once the lead singer of?

381. What rapper was questioned by the Secret Service in 2018 because in his song "Framed" about First Lady Ivanka Trump murdered in the trunk of his car.

382. Part of Interstate 10 was renamed the "Sonny Bono Highway" in 2002 in what state?

383. What rapper scored his fifth number one album in 2020 with "The Funeral"?

384. While singing her song "Tim McGraw" at the 2007 Country Music Awards, who went into the audience to introduce herself to Tim McGraw and his wife Faith Hill?

385. What rap group launched an online name generator in 2002 which turns names into ones suitable for joining the rap group?

Answers

379) "See You Again"
380) The Cranberries
381) Eminem
382) California
383) Lil' Wayne
384) Taylor Swift
385) Wu Tang Clan*

By using the Wu Tang Random Name Generator, Donald Glover took the name "Childish Gambino."

386. Bret Michaels hosted the show "Rock of Love" on VH-1 from 2007 to 2009.   What hard rock band was Michaels once the lead singer of?

387. What musical group of family members reunited for the first time in two decades to perform their 50th anniversary concert for PBS in 2007?

388. Who did Billboard magazine name as the "Artist of the Decade" for the 2010s?

389. Which member of the legendary band Kiss was the third contestant fired by Donald Trump on season seven of the "Celebrity Apprentice" in 2008?

390. Who had a number one single in February of 2012 with "Stronger (What Doesn't Kill You)"?

391. What country star set a record in the spring of 2023 when all 36 songs from his album "One Thing at a Time" landed in the Hot 100?

392. What Rapper had his second number one hit in 2022 with "Wait for U" which featured Drake and Tems?

Answers

386) Poison

387) The Osmonds

388) Drake*

389) Gene Simmons

390) Kelly Clarkson

391) Morgan Wallen

392) Future

During the decade, Drake had nine number one albums and 33 top ten singles.

393. Name the former host of "American Bandstand" who died April 18, 2012?

394. Whose third album "Loose," included the number one hits "Promiscuous," "Say in Right," and "Maneater"?

395. Which female singer became the first person in history to accumulate 100 million likes on Facebook in 2014?

396. What song by Semisonic does Justin Timberlake sing in his 2011 movie "Friends with Benefits"?

397. Name the 2016 movie accompanied by a soundtrack which featured the song "City of Stars," that won the Academy Award for Best Original Song.

398. What future superstar performed her songs "Chasing Pavements" and "Cold Shoulder" on her first appearance as the musical guest star of Saturday Night Live in 2008?

399. Who paired with Carrie Underwood on the 2014 number one hit on the country chart "Somethin' Bad"?

Answers

393) Dick Clark
395) Shakira
397) "LaLa Land"
399) Miranda Lambert

394) Nelly Furtado
396) "Closing Time"
398) Adele*

Adele's appearance coincided with Vice Presidential Candidate Sarah Palin appearing in a skit with Tina Fey, who had done very popular impressions of Palin. It was the highest rated episode in 14 years, giving Adele ample exposure.

400. Who played Johnny Cash in the 2005 film "Walk the Line"?

401. Malcolm Young died in 2017.What highly successful hard rock band did he co-found and play guitar for?

402. Name the country superstar whose 2002 album "Up!" sold 11 million albums in United States alone.

403. What boy band played their first ever show on November 18, 2011, at the Watford Colosseum in London, England?

404. What girl group stayed at number one on the U.S. Billboard hot 100 for eleven weeks with their 2001 album "Survivor"?

405. In 2021, what pop group went to number one in 19 countries with their first album in 40 years titled "Voyage"?

406. What rapper's 2011 album "Blue Slide Park" became the first independently distributed album to top the U.S. Billboard 200 in over 15 years?

Answers

400) Joaquin Phoenix

401) ACDC

402) Shania Twain

403) One Direction

404) Destiny's Child

405) ABBA*

406) Mac Miller

*"Voyage" is not only an album but also a virtual concert residency held in London, with the group appearing as they did in 1977.

407. Who, in 2001, became the first musician billionaire?

408. What rapper went to number one with her debut album in 2011 titled "Pink Friday"?

409. Name the British artist whose successful 2012 debut album included the hits "Two Fingers" and "Lightning Bolt."

410. What rapper appeared on Justin Bieber's 2010 breakout hit "Baby"?

411. In 2010, Katy Perry became the second artist to have five number one songs from the same album. Who was the first?

412. What folk singer-songwriter scored his second number one album in 2010 with "To the Sea"?

413. What music legend sang in his 2006 song "Thunder On The Mountain," "I was thinking 'bout Alicia Keys, couldn't keep from crying"?

Answers

407) Paul McCartney*
408) Nicki Minaj
409) Jake Bugg
410) Ludacris
411) Michael Jackson
412) Jack Johnson
413) Bob Dylan

*McCartney, as the writer of many of the Beatles songs, did well on the publishing rights, along with his solo hits. Also, his wife Linda was worth about $200 million when she passed away.

414. Who, in 2013, became the first musician to be named People Magazine's "Sexiest Man Alive"?

415. What is the name of the 2006 movie starring Beyonce, Jennifer Hudson, Jamie Foxx, and Eddie Murphy about fictional all female Motown group in the 1960s and 70s?

416. Name the famous saxophone player who appeared on Lady Gaga's single "The Edge of Glory" in 2011, less than two months before his death.

417. Who won the Grammy for Best Rock Song with their 2003 single "Seven Nation Army"?

418. Whose "Divide" tour was the top grossing tour of 2018?

419. Name the singer and actor who died March 20, 2020, at the age of 81 and who sold more than 100 million albums in his lifetime.

420. What country singer had a song titled "Weed with Willie" in which he vows to never smoke marijuana with country legend Wille Nelson again?

Answers

414) Adam Levine
416) Clarence Clemons*
418) Ed Sheeran
420) Toby Keith

415) "Dreamgirls"
417) The White Stripes
419) Kenny Rogers

*Clemons was a long-time member of Bruce Springsteen's "E Street Band." Gaga grew up listening to Springsteen records and was a big fan of Springsteen and Clemons. Clemons passed away on the day the music video for "The Edge of Glory" was released.

421. What music legend was honored by appearing on a U.S. postage stamp in 2008, ten years after his death?

422. What group, led by Robbie Williams, broke a record in the United Kingdom when it sold over 1.3 million concert tickets in 24 hours in 2010?

423. On what comedy-drama television series did the hip-hop group Migos play a fictional version of themselves in 2016?

424. What country music legend created a meme of herself in 2020 with representations of herself on Facebook, Linkedin, Instagram, and Tinder which was soon copied by other celebrities while going viral?

425. Who received the Grammy for "Best Male Pop Vocal Performance" in 2011 for the song "Just the Way You Are" from his debut album "Doo-Wops and Hooligans"?

426. What is the name of the 2009 song by Eminem, Dr. Dre, and 50 cent which won the Grammy for "Best Rap Performance by a Duo or Group"?

427. What superstar's fan base are known as the Arianators?

Answers

421) Frank Sinatra

422) Take That

423) "Atlanta"

424) Dolly Parton

425) Bruno Mars

426) "Crack a Bottle"*

427) Ariana Grande

*"Crack a Bottle" set a record for most digital sales in its first week by selling 418,000 units. However, that record was broken just seven days later by Flo Rida's "Right Round."

428. Whose 2000 album "No Strings Attached" broke the record for first week sales with 2.4 million copies sold?

429. What Portland, Oregon based band led by Colin McCoy was referenced in episodes of both successful comedies "The Office" and "Parks and Recreation"?

430. What country music husband and wife team embarked on their "Soul2Soul II" tour in 2006, which became the highest grossing country music tour of all time?

431. When he joined Ariana Grande to perform "Right There," Big Sean became the first rapper to perform where?

432. Name the contestant who won the second season of "American Idol" in 2003 and would later have hits with the songs "Flying Without Wings," "Sorry 2004,' and "Change Me."

433. Who did Time Magazine name as their "Entertainer of the Year" in 2021 when she was just 18 years old?

434. What rapper had his first number one album in 2005 with "Big Bang," which included "Touch It" and "In the Ghetto"?

Answers

428) NSYNC*

429) The Decemberists

430) Tim McGraw and Faith Hill

431) The White House

432) Reuben Stoddard

433) Olivia Rodrigo

434) Busta Rhymes

*The record stood for 15 years, until its first week sales were surpassed by Adele's "25."

435. Chester Bennington died of suicide on July 20, 2017. For what band, once known as Zero, was he the lead singer?

436. What Taylor Swift song broke the record for most digital sales by a female artist on August 21, 2012?

437. What band won the 2011 Grammy for "Album of the Year" with "The Suburbs"?

438. Whose 2013 song "Follow Your Arrow" was named as the 39th best country music song of all time by Rolling Stone Magazine?

439. Who sang their 1983 hit "Total Eclipse of the Heart" during a solar eclipse on August 21, 2017?

440. What pop superstar played the role of aspiring singer Billie Frank in the 2001 film "Glitter"?

441. Who had their first number one single in the U.S. in 2022 with "Unholy"?

Answers

435) Linkin Park
436) "We Are Never Getting Back Together"
437) Arcade Fire
438) Kacey Musgraves
439) Bonnie Tyler*
440) Mariah Carey
441) Sam Smith

Several musicians performed during the eclipse, including Ozzy Osbourne who performed "Bark at the Moon."

442. What rapper, despite having a previous hit titled "Cop Killer," played a police officer named Fin Tutuola on the successful television series "Law and Order"?

443. Who had their first top ten hit in 2006 with "White and Nerdy"?

444. Name the singer most known for his song "Miss Misery" from the "Good Will Hunting" soundtrack who died by suicide in 2003.

445. Who teamed with Alicia Keys in 2004 to have a number one hit with "My Boo," his fourth number one in that year?

446. What legendary band had their fourth number one hit in 2000 with "Beautiful Day"?

447. What is the title of the duet by Elton John and Dua Lipa which went to the top of the U.K. singles chart in 2021, marking John's first hit to top the charts there in 16 years?

448. Name the former star of "The Partridge Family" who died November 21, 2017?

Answers

442) Ice-T *

443) Weird Al Yankovic

444) Elliot Smith

445) Usher

446) U2

447) "Cold Heart"

448) David Cassidy

*The song "Cop Killer" was released in 1992 just weeks before the L.A. riots in the wake of the Rodney King verdict. It drew considerable backlash from multiple sources, including President George H.W. Bush. Ultimately, Ice-T removed the song from the album "Body Count."

449. What rapper teamed with Rihanna on the number one hit "The Monster" in 2013?

450. In the year 2000, The Chicago Sun was the first news organization to publish court documents regarding allegations about what hip hop star having sexual relationships with underage girls?

451. Who was the highest earning performer of 2008, largely because of her "Sticky and Sweet" tour?

452. Name the country-rap song released in 2019 which has sold 18 million units worldwide, making it one of the best-selling singles of all time?

453. Whose song "Home" became the best-selling song in the history of "American Idol" after he won its eleventh season in 2012?

454. Name the 2016 hit by Beyonce that begins with "Y'all haters corny with that Illuminati mess, Paparazzi, catch my fly, and my cocky fresh."

455. Who, in 2015 became the first female country music singer to have her debut single reach number one since Carrie Underwood did it nearly a decade earlier?

Answers

449) Eminem
451) Madonna
453) Phillip Phillips
455) Kelsea Ballerini

450) R. Kelly
452) "Old Town Road"
454) "Formation"*

*In 2021, Rolling Stone Magazine named "Formation" as the greatest music video of all time.

456. Although the two never married, what superstar had a decade long relationship with soccer star Gerard Pique, which included having two children together?

457. Name the Canadian born rock legend who pulled all his music from the streaming service Spotify because they carried "The Joe Rogan Experience," who the artist felt was spreading false information about the dangers of the covid-19 vaccine.

458. What band had commercial success as well as critical acclaim with their debut album "Hot Fuss" released in 2004?

459. Who released the album "Sob Rock" in July of 2021, their first studio album in four years?

460. The engagement between Jennifer Lopez and what actor was called off on January 22, 2004?

461. Whose Grammy nominated rap song "Swimming Pools (Drank)" was featured on 2014's "Grand Theft Auto V"?

462. What band, named after an important figure in history, had their breakout hit in 2004 with "Take Me Out"?

Answers

456) Shakira
458) The Killers
460) Ben Affleck
462) Franz Ferdinand*

457) Neil Young
459) John Mayer
461 Kendrick Lamar

*It was the assassination of Archduke Franz Ferdinand, heir to the Austro-Hungarian throne, by a Serbian nationalist which sparked the beginning of World War One.

463. Who became the first K-pop band to have a number one album in the U.S. with "Love Yourself: Tear"?

464. What rock legend was the airport in Liverpool, England, named after in 2001?

465. Name the country music legend who was nominated for an Academy Award for Best Original song for his 2014 release "I'm Not Gonna Miss You" about his battle with Alzheimer's disease.

466. As of June 2023, who is the only female rapper ever to have five number one singles?

467. What is the name of the band comprised of Jack Black and Kyle Gass who the 2006 movie "The Pick of Destiny" was based upon?

468. In 2014, Katy Perry was the most streamed female artist on Spotify. Who was the most streamed male artist?

469. Name the former lead singer of the Stone Temple Pilots and Velvet Revolver who died of a cardiac arrest in 2015 on his tour bus.

Answers

463) BTS

464) John Lennon

465) Glen Campbell*

466) Cardi B

467) "Tenacious D"

468) Ed Sheeran

469) Scott Weiland

The song is from the soundtrack of Campbell's documentary "I'll Be Me" which focuses on his battle with Alzheimer's and last tour. He was unable to perform it at the Academy Award ceremony, so Tim McGraw filled in.

470. What legendary hard rock band played their last concert in 2017, which ended with a performance of their first big hit "Paranoid"?

471. What star was formally released by a judge from a Conservatorship with her father in November of 2021?

472. Released in 2021, what rapper's "The Off-Season" became his sixth number one album?

473. What singer became the first ever male to appear on the cover of Vogue Magazine in December 2019?

474. In 2019, what all-time great rap group had a section of New York's Staten Island named after them?

475. Whose "Flip-Flop Summer" tour was the highest grossing country music tour of 2007?

476. What hip hop star had both the number one song and number one album in America for seven consecutive weeks in 2016?

Answers

470) Black Sabbath
472) J. Cole
474) Wu Tang Clan
476) Drake*

471) Britney Spears
473) Harry Styles
475) Kenny Chesney

*With the song "One Dance" from the album "Views," Drake tied the record held by Michael Jackson for the song "Billie Jean" from the album "Thriller."

477. Who teamed with Halsey in 2016 on the number one hit "Closer"?

478. The highest grossing music festival was 2019's "Outside Lands" in what state?

479. What rapper teamed with Martha Stewart to begin hosting a cooking show on VH1 in 2016?

480. What band announced they were getting back together at the 2009 Grammy Awards, about four months after a plane crash nearly killed their drummer, Travis Barker?

481. What rock legend won a Tony in 2003 for his orchestration of the musical "Movin' Out"?

482. Who won a Grammy in 2013 for Best Country Duo/Group Performance for their hit single "Pontoon"?

483. Lemmy died on December 28, 2015. For what Heavy Metal band did he serve as the front man, and only continuous member of?

Answers

477) The Chainsmokers

478) California

479) Snoop Dogg*

480) Blink-182

481) Billy Joel

482) Little Big Town

483) Motorhead

*In 2023, at the age of 81, Stewart became the oldest model to appear in Sports Illustrated's annual swimsuit issue.

484. Who had his first number one single in 2021 when he teamed with Lil Nas on "Industry Baby"?

485. Who surpassed Elvis Presley in 2015 to become the solo artist with the most albums sold in the history of the United States?

486. What is the name of the 2003 hit by 50 Cent which begins with the line "Go, go, go shorty, it's your birthday?

487. Who released their second studio album in 2021, titled "Happier Than Ever"?

488. What young star caused a stir in 2013 when he wrote in the guest book at the Anne Frank Museum in Amsterdam that he hoped Ms. Frank would have been a fan?

489. Who played their last concert on April 14, 2016, in Atlanta, then died a week later?

490. Who, in 2018, became the first African American woman to headline the Coachella Festival?

Answers

484) Jack Harlow

485) Garth Brooks

486) "In Da Club"

487) Billie Eilish

488) Justin Bieber

489) Prince

490) Beyonce

*Bieber wrote in the guest book "Truly inspiring to be able to come here. Anne was a great girl. Hopefully she would have been a Belieber.

491. Who topped the chart in 2006 with their Ninth studio album "Stadium Arcadium"?

492. Name the musician, dead since 1980, whose circular glasses sparked an online bidding war in 2007.

493. Who had an international hit with her song "There You'll Be" from the Soundtrack of the 2001 film "Pearl Harbor"?

494. Name the song by Post Malone and Swan Lee from the soundtrack of the 2018 film "Spider-Man: Into the Spider-Verse" which stayed in the top ten for 33 weeks.

495. What was the title of the Adele album which was the best-selling album of 2015?

496. Whose 2003 "Black Album" included the hits "99 Problems," Dirt Off Your Shoulder," and "Change Clothes"?

497. Who, at the age of 67, in 2008 became the oldest artist to have a number one album on the U.S. chart with his release "Home Before Dark"?

Answers

491) The Red Hot Chili Peppers 492) John Lennon
493) Faith Hill 494) "Sunflower"
495) "25" 496) Jay-Z
497) Neil Diamond*

Diamond broke the record previusly held by Bob Dylan, whose "Modern Times" topped the chart in 2006.

498. In 2018, what Guns N' Roses video became the first from the 1990s to surpass one billion views on YouTube?

499. What superstar did Ashton Kutcher prank on the very first episode of MTV's "Punked" in 2003?

500. Who won their first Grammy for their 2019 album "Igor," which won for Best Rap Album?

501. What Shakira song, which featured Wyclef Jean, broke the record for most plays on American radio stations in a single week in 2014?

502. Prince Markie Dee passed away in 2018. What pioneering rap group from the 1980s was he a member of?

503. What popular 2001 film featured the band Smashmouth's cover of "I'm a Believer" as the credits rolled?

504. What song by the band Journey was performed on the first episode of "Glee" in 2009?

Answers

498) "November Rain"

499) Justin Timberlake

500) Tyler, The Creator

501) "Hips Don't Lie"

502) The Fat Boys

503) "Shrek"

504) "Don't Stop Believin'"*

The Glee version reached number four on the pop chart, five spots higher than Journey's original version peaked.

505. Whose 2011 album, their fifth, titled "Mylo Xyloto" went to number one in over thirty countries?

506. In 2015, what album became the first to sell more than thirty million copies in the United States, 33 years after it was released?

507. Who replaced Gwen Stefani as a coach on "The Voice" in 2016?

508. Who made history in 2022 when they had all top ten songs on the Billboard "Hot 100" chart?

509. Michael Andres featuring Gary Jules had a number one song on the U.K. singles chart with a cover of a Tears for Fears song that appeared on the "Donnie Darko" movie soundtrack. Name the song.

510. On what song did Jimmy Buffett duet with Alan Jackson to have a number one hit on the country chart in 2003?

511. What band released their "Teal" album in 2019 which included covers of "Take on Me," "No Scrubs," and "Africa"?

Answers

505) Coldplay

506) "Thriller"

507) Christina Aguilera

508) Taylor Swift*

509) "Mad World"

510) "Its Five O'clock Somewhere"

511) Weezer

*The feat happened after her album "Midnights" was released in October 2022. She surpassed Drake, who had nine of the top ten songs during 2021.

512. What duo won the Grammy for Best Alternative Music album in 2008 for "Icky Thump"?

513. What Queen song was the most Googled song of 2018?

514. In what year did streaming services first take over the lead in total sales over CDs and vinyl records?

515. What singer became the first non-athlete to have a banner hung in his honor at New York's Madison Square Garden in 2006?

516. Who, in 2011, released the album "4" as her fourth album, because it is her favorite number, and because she was born September 4 and married on April 4?

517. "Let It Go" from the movie "Frozen" won the Academy Award for Best Original Song in 2014. Who sang it?

518. What superstar played the role of "Nine Ball" in the 2018 film "Ocean's 8"?

Answers

512) The White Stripes
514) 2018
516) Beyonce
518) Rihanna

513) "Bohemian Rhapsody"
515) Billy Joel*
517) Idina Menzel

Joel has since been joined by musicians Elton John, Harry Styles, and the band Phish in the rafters at Madison Square Garden.

519. Whose album "Voodoo," released in the year 2000, debuted at number one in the U.S. and included the Grammy winning single "Untitled (How Does it Feel)"?

520. Name the singer of hits such as "Addicted to Love," "Bad Case of Loving You," and "I Didn't mean to Turn You On" who was found dead in a Paris hotel room on September 26, 2003.

521. What deceased singer had a park named after him in 2011 near the house he grew up in in Aberdeen, Washington?

522. What band tied a record by winning nine Grammy Awards for their 2004 album "How to Dismantle an Atomic Bomb"?

523. What 2017 song became the first song sung mostly in Spanish to reach number one since "The Macarena" achieved that feat in 1996?

524. What was the name of the short-form video platform which helped launch the careers of several prominent artists, including Shawn Mendes, which was discontinued by Twitter in 2015?

525. Who became the first person to be named as Spotify's most streamed artist three years in a row, from 2020-2022?

Answers

519) D'Angelo

520) Robert Palmer

521) Kurt Cobain

522) U2

523) "Despacato"

524) Vine

525) Bad Bunny*

*In both 2021 and 2022 Taylor Swift finished second to Bad Bunny. Rounding out the top five for 2022 were Drake, The Weeknd, and BTS.

526. Whose 4ᵗʰ studio album "Confessions" was named 2004's "Album of the Year" by Billboard Magazine?

527. In August of 2018, to whom did Aerosmith lead singer Steven Tyler send a letter demanding that the person "Cease and Desist" using Aerosmith songs at his Presidential campaign rallies?

528. Who had a number one hit in 2007 with "Hey There Delilah"?

529. Who was named the "World's Richest Drummer" in 2012?

530. What Chicago based band was the subject of the 2002 documentary "I Am Trying to Break Your Heart"?

531. Who broke his own record for longest concert by one artist in the United States by playing for four hours and four minutes on September 8ᵗʰ and 9ᵗʰ, 2016?

532. What rapper made a cameo appearance in the 2010 film "Hawaii 5-0" as Gordon Smith, the character named as a "person of interest" in a murder case?

Answers

526) Usher

527) Donald Trump

528) Plain White T's*

529) Ringo Starr

530) Wilco

531) Bruce Springsteen

532) Nas

*The song was written by lead singer Tom Higgenson, who was attracted to Delilah DiCrescenzo, a steeplechase runner he had met through a friend. She was not interested, as she was already dating someone.

533. What country singer reached number one with his debut album "Traveller," released in 2015?

534. Name the musician who was in the original class of inductees into the Rock and Roll Hall of Fame and was rescued from the flooding caused by Hurricane Katrina in New Orleans in 2005.

535. What pop superstar joined Maroon Five on their smash hit "Moves Like Jagger" in 2010?

536. What alternative band had their first number one album with their sixth one, titled "Showroom of Compassion" in 2011?

537. What hard rock band became the only band to play on all seven continents, with each continent being played in the year 2013?

538. What young rapper starred in the 2023 remake of the film "White Men Can't Jump"?

539. Who joined Robin Thicke to perform his song at the MTV Video Music Awards in 2013, which drew a formal complaint from the Parents Television Council for the suggestive nature of their dancing?

Answers

533) Chris Stapleton

534) Fats Domino

535) Christina Aguilera

536) Cake

537) Metallica*

538) Jack Harlow

539) Miley Cyrus

*On December 8, 2013, Metallica played a one hour concert dubbed "Freeze 'Em All" in a small dome in Antarctica. The 120 fans in attendance were contest winners flown in from all over the world.

540. Whose 2014 song "Bailando" spent 41 weeks on top of Billboard's "Hot Latin Songs" chart?

541. What band scored a top ten hit with their cover of the Talk Talk song "It's My Life" in 2003?

542. In 2020, who became the first artist ever to have three singles debut at number one on the hot 100 chart in less than a year when his single "Franchise" reached the top spot.

543. As of July 2023, who has more Instagram followers than any other male musician?

544. Whose "American Kids" did Rolling Stone Magazine name the best country song of 2014?

545. Who became the oldest woman ever to win the Grammy for "Song of the Year" in 2023 when she won it with her single "Just Like That"?

546. What rapper celebrated the 25th anniversary of his marriage to model Mandy Aragones in 2022?

Answers

540) Enrique Iglesias*
542) Travis Scott
544) Kenny Chesney
546) Slick Rick

541) No Doubt
543) Justin Bieber
545) Bonnie Raitt

Enrique is the son of Julio Iglesias the most commercially successful Spanish artist of all time.

547. Name the country music star who not only released a song called "Beer for My Horses," but also starred in a 2008 movie of the same name.

548. Whose 2006 album "FutureSex/LoveSounds" became the biggest selling album for pre-sales in the history of iTunes?

549. What legendary band had a number two album in both the U.S. and U.K. in 2002 with "Forty Licks"?

550. A hologram of which late rapper famously performed alongside the live Snoop Dogg and Dr. Dre at the Coachella Music Festival in 2012?

551. In 2016, when Pearl Jam front man Eddie Vedder's favorite baseball team reached their first World Series in over seven decades, he sang "Take Me Out to the Ballgame" for them during the seventh inning stretch. What team was that?

552. What artist was pelted with kiwifruit at a 2017 concert in Manchester, England by the crowd when he sang his hit "Kiwi"?

553. Name the popular show about hip hop mogul Lucious Lyon which aired on the Fox network from 2015 to 2020?

Answers

547) Toby Keith

548) Justin Timberlake

549) The Rolling Stones

550) Tupac Shakur

551) The Chicago Cubs*

552) Harry Styles

553) "Atlanta"

*Vedder is a lifelong Cubs fan. He had a long friendship with "Mr. Cub" Ernie Banks and partied with the team in the clubhouse after their historic World Series victory.

554. Whose 2007 album "Dreaming Out Loud" included the smash hits "Apologize" and "Stop and Stare"?

555. Name the "American Idol" season five winner whose single "Do I Make You Proud" debuted at Number One on the Billboard chart in 2006?

556. What fellow country music star was Miranda Lambert married to from 2011 to 2015?

557. Who earned her second consecutive Grammy Award for "Best Female R and B Vocal Performance" in 2009 for "Superwoman"?

558. Who achieved his sixth top ten hit in 2020 when he released the duet titled "Monster" with Justin Bieber?

559. What is the 21st century music star who was born Stefani Germanotta better known as?

560. Whose "Super Bass" was the most streamed song of 2011?

Answers

554) One Republic

555) Taylor Hicks

556) Blake Shelton

557) Alicia Keys

558) Shawn Mendes

559) Lady Gaga*

560) Nicki Minaj

*The name "Lady Gaga" was chosen because of the song "Radio Ga Ga" by Queen.

561. In 2023, which song by the Beatles became their first to reach a billion streams on Spotify?

562. Cardi B announced she was pregnant with her child named Kulture during a 2018 performance on Saturday Night Live. What rapper is Kulture's father?

563. What female singer's album "No Angel" was the best-selling album of 2001?

564. Whose 2013 album "Midnight Memories" debuted at number one, making them the first group to have their first three albums debut in the top spot?

565. Although it was their third overall album, whose album "Cuz I Love You," which was their major label debut, burst them into stardom in 2019?

566. What first season of which reality series that first appeared on MTV in 2001 was the most watched series on the history of that network at the time?

567. Who received the Country Music Association award for "single of the year" for their 2000 hit "I Hope You Dance"?

Answers

561) "Here Comes the Sun"*

562) Offset

563) Dido

564) One Direction

565) Lizzo

566) "The Osbournes"

567) Lee Ann Womack

*As of June, 2023, there have been 419 songs which have been streamed a billion times on Spotify.

568. What singer from Ravendale, Washington won the 2023 Grammy for "Best Rock Song" for her single, "Broken Horses"?

569. What band had two hits in the top five at the same time in 2016 with "Heathens" and "Ride"?

570. What Swedish DJ, remixer, and producer died by suicide at the age of 28 on April 20, 2018?

571. What band, who was virtually unknown at the time, had a number one hit in 2013 with "We are Young" after it appeared on the popular series "Glee"?

572. What competitive singing show debuted on NBC on April 26, 2011?

573. What singer and actress has been married to both Ryan Adams and Taylor Gouldsmith, lead singer of the band Dawes?

574. What rapper, singer, producer and songwriter was featured in both the hits "Promiscuos" by Nelly Furtado and "Cry Me a River" by Justin Timberlake?

Answers

568) Brandi Carlile

569) Twenty One Pilots

570) Avicii

571) F.U.N.

572) "The Voice"

573) Mandy Moore

574) Timbaland*

*The name "Timbaland" comes from producer DeVante Swing's mispronunciation of the shoe brand.

575. Who had a number one country hit with his 2015 release "Die a Happy Man"?

576. For what 2002 movie did actress and musician Queen Latifah receive an academy award nomination for best supporting actress for her portrayal of the character Matron "Mama" Morton?

577. What hip hop star played "The Love Doctor" on a 2002 episode of "Sabrina the Teenage Witch"?

578. Released in 2010, "Whip My Hair" was a hit by what ten-year-old singer who is the child of a prominent actor and rapper?

579. Whose 2007 album "Spirit" is the best-selling debut album by a female artist in the history of the United Kingdom?

580. What artist is the subject of the 2009 film "Notorious"?

581. Name the Chicago based band known for its quirky and original music videos who won the Grammy for Best Music Video for their 2007 hit "Here It Goes Again."

Answers

575) Thomas Rhett*

576) "Chicago"

577) Usher

578) Willow Smith

579) Leona Lewis

580) Notorious B.I.G.

581) O.K. Go

The song was written for Rhett's wife, Lauren, who he has known since the first grade.

582. Darius Rucker had a number one country hit in 2013 with his cover of a song by Old Crow Medicine Show. What is the name of that song?

583. Who famously performed at the 2001 MTV Video Music Awards with a python draped around her shoulders?

584. Name the Jamaican born singer and rapper who had number one hits early in the 21st century with "Get Busy" and "Temperature"?

585. What superstar's real name is Robyn Fenty?

586. What singer reached the top of the Country music chart with her 2004 single, "Redneck Woman"?

587. Who paired with Megan Thee Stallion in 2020 to have a number one hit with "Wap"?

588. Name the native of Mississippi who released her hit country single "Mississippi Girl" just a few weeks before the state was ravaged by Hurricane Katrina in 2005?

Answers

582) "Wagon Wheel"*
583) Britney Spears
584) Sean Paul
585) Rihanna
586) Gretchen Wilson
587) Cardi B
588) Faith Hill"

Bob Dylan and Ketcham Secor share the writing credits for "Wagon Wheel." The "Rock Me Mama" chorus comes from a Dylan Bootleg. The lyrics of that bootleg were nearly impossible to understand. Secor, who was 17 at the time, re-wrote the lyrics into what was recorded by Old Crow Medicine Show and later Darius Rucker.

589. What female artist joined Pitbull on his top ten hit from 2011 titled "Feel This Moment"?

590. What metal band won the Grammy for Best Hard Rock Performance in 2006 for "B.Y.O.B."?

591. What rapper died of an accidental fentanyl overdose at a friend's house in Los Angeles in 2022 at the age of 59?

592. What movie soundtrack won six awards at the 2002 Grammys, more than any individual artist did that year?

593. Who broke Elvis Presley's record for most number one hits in the United States by a solo artist in 2008?

594. Who had their first number one country hit in 2001 with "But for the Grace of God"?

595. What boy band released the song "Glad You Came" in 2011, which went to number one in the U.K. and number three in the U.S.?

Answers

589) Christina Aguilera
590) System of a Down
591) Coolio
592) "O' Brother Where Art Thou"
593) Mariah Carey*
594) Keith Urban
595) The Wanted

Carey has the most for a solo artist, while the Beatles have the most of any band, with 20.

596. The Destiny's Child song "Independent Women Part One" stayed at number one for 11 consecutive weeks in 2000 and 2001. What movie from the year 2000 starring Cameron Diaz, Drew Barrymore, and Lucy Liu was it featured on the soundtrack of?

597. What famous lead singer for a Rock and Roll inducted band broke his leg during a show in Sweden but returned to the stage to play 24 more songs and finish the set that night in 2015?

598. Who was named the country music entertainer of the year in both 2021 and 2022 at the Country Music Association's award show?

599. Name the Las Vegas based rock band which was the first to have four different songs streamed a billion times each on Spotify.

600. What song by Snoop Dogg, featuring Pharrell was named by Billboard Magazine as the most popular rap song of the decade in 2009?

601. In what year was the iTunes music store opened by Apple?

602. Who won a Grammy for both Song of the Year and Best Pop Solo Performance for their 2014 single "Thinking Out Loud"?

Answers

596) "Charlie's Angels"
597) Dave Grohl (Foo Fighters)*
598) Luke Combs
599) Imagine Dragons
600) "Drop it Like It's Hot"
601) 2003
602) Ed Sheeran

Grohl was taken backstage for several minutes while the band played David Bowie and Queen's "Under Pressure." Grohl finished the show with a doctor on stage holding his leg, and then finished the tour while playing from a specially designed throne while his leg recovered with a plate and several pins in it.

603. What 2011 Coldplay song had a video in which lead vocalist Chris Martin dressed as an elephant trying to find its way home, which won "Best Rock Video" at the 2012 MTV Video Music Awards?

604. Whose "Back to Bedlam" album was the best-selling album in the U.K. in the 2000s?

605. Kelis had a top three hit in 2003 singing about what beverage?

606. Name the band from Iceland that hat hits in the 2010s with "Little Talks, "King and Lionheart," and "Mountain Sound."

607. What singer received a nomination for the Academy Award for Best Supporting Actress for her portrayal Florence Jackson in the 2017 film "Mudbound"?

608. Name the 2015 hit by Justin Bieber that begins with the lyrics "For all the times that you rained on my parade, and all the clubs you got into using my name."

609. Lady Gaga and Ariana Grande became the first all-female duo or group to win the Grammy for Best Pop Duo/Group Performance in 2021.   What was the name of the song they won it for?

Answers

603) "Paradise"   604) James Blunt*
605) "Milkshake"   606) Of Monsters and Men
607) Mary J. Blige   608) "Love Yourself"
609) "Rain on Me"

*Blunt served in the British military for four years, which included an assignment with N.A.T.O. in the war in Kosovo in the late 1990s.

610. "I'm Not There" is a 2007 film about the life and music of what rock and folk legend?

611. Name the former "American Idol" contestant country singer who won the 16th season of "Dancing with the Stars" with her partner Derek Hough in 2013.

612. For which single did Billie Eilish win the Grammy for both Record of the Year and Song of the year at the 62nd Grammy Awards in 2020?

613. Whose 2010 hit "Dancing on My Own" was ranked by Rolling Stone Magazine at number 20 on their list of the 500 Greatest Songs of All Time?

614. Name the country singer whose 5th album, titled "Fifth Gear," was released in 2007 and included four singles which reached number one on the Hot Country Chart.

615. What song by Lady Gaga and Beyonce was the fourth best-selling song of 2010?

616. What is the rock duo comprised of Dan Auerbach and Patrick Carney better known as?

Answers

610) Bob Dylan

611) Kellie Pickler

612) "Bad Guy" *

613) Robyn

614) Brad Paisley

615) "Telephone"

616) The Black Keys

*"Bad Guy" spent nine weeks at nummber two behind "Old Town Road" before reaching the top spot, breaking the record for most weeks at number two before becoming a number one single.

617. What band received an Oscar Nomination for their song "Accidentally in Love" which was featured in the 2004 film "Shrek 2"?

618. What hard rock band had a top three hit in the year 2000 with their debut single "Kryptonite"?

619. What rapper had their first number one hit in 2018 with "Sicko Mode"?

620. Who became the youngest artist ever to be named the Country Music Association's "Entertainer of the Year" in 2011, at the age of 19?

621. Who had their seventh top ten hit in 2013 with "Treasure"?

622. Whose fourth studio album, released in 2020, titled "After Hours" had all 14 of its tracks appear in the Billboard Hot 100 chart at some point?

623. What late superstar musician and actress did Alicia Keys induct into the Rock and Roll Hall of Fame in 2020?

Answers

617) Counting Crows
619) Travis Scott
621) Bruno Mars
623) Whitney Houston

618) 3 Doors Down
620) Taylor Swift
622) The Weeknd*

*The Weeknd dropped the 'e' from his name because he feared it would cause copywrite problems with the Canadian band "The Weekend."

624. The 2016 Documentary film "Supersonic" was about which band that included brothers Noel and Liam Gallagher?

625. The original singer and co-writer of the all-time classic "Stand by Me" died April 30, 2015. Name him.

626. What is the name of the former C.E.O. of Death Row Records who pled no contest to voluntary manslaughter charges in 2018 and will not be eligible for parole until 2034?

627. What is the name of the song about the September 11, 2001, attacks by Daryl Worley which stayed at number one on the Hot Country Chart for seven weeks in 2003?

628. Who had a hit with the song "Young and Beautiful," which was featured in the 2013 movie "The Great Gatsby"?

629. What is the name of the first daughter born to Kanye West and Kim Kardashian on June 15, 2013?

630. Who won the Grammy for "Best Dance Recording" in 2000 for her hit single "Believe"?

Answers

624) Oasis

625) Ben E. King

626) Suge Knight*

627) "Have You Forgotten?"

628) Lana Del Rey

629) North West

630) Cher

*Knight was once an accomplished football player. He played at the University of Nevada Las Vegas in the mid-1980s and appeared in two games as a replacement player for the Los Angeles Rams during the 1987 NFL player's strike.

631. What Queen song won the title of "most played at sporting events" according to Musicraiser.com in 2019?

632. What N.F.L. player became even more famous after he began dating Taylor Swift in 2023?

633. Whose 2002 debut studio album "Let it Go" is the best-selling album in the 21st century by any Canadian artist?

634. What country singer had their first number one country hit with his debut single "What Was I Thinkin'" in 2003?

635. What Alicia Keys hit includes the lyrics "Looks like a girl, but she's a flame. So bright, she can burn your eyes"?

636. What hip hop star married his longtime girlfriend Keyshia Ka'oir in a nationally televised, star-studded event in 2017?

637. What superstar caused an international uproar when he dangled his nine month old baby over a hotel balcony in Germany in 2002?

Answers

631) "We Will Rock You"*
632) Travis Kelce
633) Avril Lavigne
634) Dierks Bentley
635) "Girl on Fire"
636) Gucci Mane
637) Michael Jackson

Other songs at the top of the list of most played at sporting events include "Crazy Train," "Seven Nation Army," "Welcome to the Jungle," "We are the Champions," and "Centerfield."

638. Whose 2015 performance at half time of the Super Bowl left America talking about the background dancer who would become known as "Left Shark"?

639. Tom Hanks played "Colonel" Tom Parker in a 2022 biopic of what legendary musician?

640. A star-studded celebration was held at the Hollywood Bowl on April 29th and 30th, 2023 to celebrate the 90th birthday(s) of what country music legend?

641. What fruit did Gwen Stefani help listeners remember the spelling of in her 2005 hit "Hollaback Girl"?

642. 23 people were killed in a 2017 bombing in Manchester, England following a concert by what pop superstar?

643. What popular hard rock band finally released the album "Chinese Democracy" in 2008, after 15 years of promising it?

644. What rapper joined Dr. Dre on the hit from the year 2000 "Forgot About Dre"?

Answers

638) Katy Perry

639) Elvis Presley

640) Willie Nelson*

641) Bananas

642) Ariana Grande

643) Guns and Roses

644) Eminem

*Nelson was born right before midnight on April 29, but the birth was not registered in the county courthouse until the next day. There is dispute about which day his actual birthday should be, but Willie Nelson simply celebrates both days.

645. Name the former lead singer of the band Whiskeytown whose 2001 album "Gold" was rated as the 81st best album of the 2000s by Rolling Stone Magazine.

646. Who, in 2023, became the first female hip hop artist inducted into the Rock and Roll Hall of Fame?

647. Name the American Indie-Rock band formed in 2002 in Middletown, Connecticut who had a top ten hit in 2007 with their song "Kids."

648. Name the father-daughter duo that became the second father-daughter duo of all time to have a number one hit on the U.K. singles chart with their 2003 remake of the Black Sabbath song "Changes."

649. What hip hop star made their film debut as the voice of the character "Bufo" in the 2013 animated action fantasy movie "Epic"?

650. What future member of the Highwomen had her breakout country single in 2016 with "My Church"?

651. Who had a number one hit in 2008 with his song "All Summer Long," which sampled songs by Bob Seger, Warren Zevon, and Lynyrd Skynyrd?

Answers

645) Ryan Adams*
647) MGMT
649) Pitbull
651) Kid Rock

646) Missy Elliot
648) Kelly and Ozzy Osbourne
650) Maren Morris

*Adams is often confused with Canadian pop star Bryan Adams. Ironically, they share November 5th birthdays. Bryan was born in 1959, Ryan in 1974.

652. What rapper had his first number one hit in April 2020 with "The Scotts"?

653. What duo led an industry show of support for same sex marriage at the 2014 Grammys by performing their hit "Same Love" to accompany a mass wedding of both hetero and homosexual couples at the show?

654. What country music star was performing when the mass shooting began at the 2017 Route 91 Harvest Music Festival?

655. What legendary band ended their "360" tour in 2014, which sold more tickets and made more money than any tour in previous history?

656. Whose tribute to football titled "The Boys of the Fall" was a top twenty country hit in 2010?

657. What country music legend made several appearances as Hannah's aunt on the series "Hannah Montana"?

658. Name the 2004 hit by Green Day which begins with the lyrics "I walk a lonely road, the only one that I have known. Don't know where it goes, but its home to me."

Answers

652) Kid Cudi

653) Macklemore and Ryan Lewis

654) Jason Aldean

655) U2

656) Kenny Chesney

657) Dolly Parton

658) "Boulevard of Broken Dreams"*

*"Boulevard of Broken Dreams is also the title of a famous painting by Gottfried Helnwein featuring Marilyn Monroe, Humphrey Bogart, James Dean and Elvis Presley hanging out in a bar.

659. What singer teamed with Charlie Puth for a top ten hit in 2016 with "We Don't Talk Anymore"?

660. In 2002, what singer was named by Forbes Magazine as the most powerful celebrity in the world, despite being only 20 years old at the time?

661. Name the indie rock band from Long Beach, California who have had hits in the 21st century with "First," "So Tied Up," and "Hang Me Up to Dry."

662. Name the legendary guitarist who was inducted into the Rock and Roll Hall of Fame with both the Yardbirds and as a solo artist who died due to viral meningitis on January 10, 2023.

663. Name the band originally from Wasilla, Alaska who won the Grammy for "Best Pop Duo/Group Performance" for their 2017 single "Feel It Still."

664. Which Harry Styles hi features a child saying "Go on Harry, we want to say goodnight to you"?

665. What band had their fourth number one country hit in 2005 with "Fast Cars and Freedom"?

Answers

659) Selena Gomez
661) Cold War Kids
663) Portugal. The Man
665) Rascal Flatts

660) Britney Spears
662) Jeff Beck
664) "As it Was"*

The child's voice heard in the song is that of the five-year-old Goddaughter of Styles, who is the daughter of British producer Ben Winston.

666. "Dancing With the Devil" is a four-part documentary released in 2021 about the life and career of what singer, songwriter, and actor?

667. Whose album "The Massacre" was named the 2005 album of the year by Billboard Magazine?

668. What young pop star was stopped by authorities in a German airport in 2013 when he tried to smuggle his pet monkey into the country?

669. What superstar singer and actress played a stripper named Ramona in the 2019 movie "Hustlers"?

670. What rapper received eight Grammy nominations for his 2022 album "Mr. Morale and the Big Steppers"?

671. What band won a Grammy for Best Country Album for their 2011 release "Own the Night"?

672. What tour, sponsored by the shoe company Vans, had its final concert in Mountain View, California in 2019?

Answers

666) Demi Lovato
668) Justin Bieber
670) Kendrick Lamar
672) The Warped Tour

667) 50 Cent
669) Jennifer Lopez
671) Lady A*

Lady A was known as Lady Antebellum, but changed their the name to Lady A in 2020 in the wake of protests over the death of George Floyd to disassociate themselves from the time period of slavery in the American South.

673. What band's 2000 album "Chocolate Starfish and the Hot Dog Flavored Water" set a record for most sales by a rock record in the first week of its release?

674. Who was the best-selling artist of the 2010s in both the United States and worldwide?

675. Who had their first number one country hit in 2006 with "Jesus, Take the Wheel"?

676. BTS became the first K-Pop band to perform on what show on April 13, 2019?

677. The International Federation of Phonographic Industry shifted all global music releases to what day of the week in 2015?

678. What artist released his albums "Endless" and "Blonde" on consecutive days in 2016?

679. The video for what 2017 song became the first to receive 5 billion views on YouTube?

Answers

673) Limp Bizkit
674) Adele
675) Carrie Underwood
676) Saturday Night Live
677) Friday*
678) Frank Ocean
679) "Despacito"

*Previously, all new music had been released on Tuesday in the United States, while being released on different days throughout the world. This practice lent itself to piracy, which was the driving reason behind having all new music released on Friday throughout the world.

680. Whose 2016 album "A Sailor's Guide to the Earth" won the Grammy for "Best Country Album"?

681. "Get Back" is a critically acclaimed, eight-hour documentary about what legendary band?

682. Name the popular American rock band formed in Las Vegas in 2001 led by front man Brandon Flowers.

683. Whose 2011 album "Tailgates and Tanlines" included three number one country hits: "I Don't Want This Night to End," Drunk on You," and "Kiss Tomorrow Goodbye"?

684. What band's 2001 single "Drops of Jupiter" stayed in the Billboard Top 40 for 29 weeks?

685. What American indie-rock band won the Grammy for "Best Alternative Music Album" in 2018 for their seventh studio album, "Sleep Well Beast"?

686. The cast of what 21st century show holds the record for artist with the most top 100 hits on the Billboard chart?

Answers

680) Sturgill Simpson

681) The Beatles

682) The Killers

683) Luke Bryan

684) Train

685) The National

686) "Glee"*

As of August 2023, the cast of "Glee" has had 207 top 100 hits, surpassing Lil Wayne (127) and Elvis Presley (108.)

687. What T.V. legend stepped in to replace Dick Clark on "Dick Clark's Rockin Eve" after Clark had a stroke in 2004?

688. Whose debut single "TiK ToK" stayed at number one for nine consecutive weeks on the Billboard chart in 2010?

689. Marilyn Manson appeared in the role of Ron Tully, a white supremacist in the final season of what popular television series in 2014?

690. In 2015, Benji Madden married actress Cameron Diaz. What band is Madden the lead singer of?

691. Who sang the Etta James song "At Last" as Michelle and Barack Obama shared their first dance together as President and First Lady at an Inauguration Ball in 2009?

692. Name the singer whose "Bat Out of Hell" was one of the best-selling albums of all time who died on January 20, 2022.

693. What song from the "High School Musical" soundtrack, sang by Zac Efron, Vanessa Hudgens, and Drew Seeley became a top five hit in 2006?

Answers

687) Regis Philbin

688) Kesha

689) "Sons of Anarchy"

690) Good Charlotte

691) Beyonce

692) Meat Loaf

693) "Breaking Free"*

*"Breaking Free" debuted at number 86 on the Billboard chart, but leaped to number four in its second week on the chart, marking the biggest jump in one week in Billboard history.

694. What legendary rap group was Flavor Flav kicked out of on March 1, 2020?

695. What music icon donated One Million Dollars in 2020 to the Vanderbilt University Medical Center to help fund research for a coronavirus vaccine?

696. What hard rock band had their only top ten hit in 2001 with "It's Been Awhile" off their third album, "Break the Cycle"?

697. What singer achieved his first country number one single with the title track to his 2011 album "Barefoot Blue Jean Night"?

698. What music superstar played the role of Napster founder Sean Parker in the 2010 movie "The Social Network" about the founding of Facebook?

699. Which of the Jonas Brothers was married at a palace in India on December 1, 2018?

700. Name the artist whose 2002 album titled "Up" made her the only female artist to have three consecutive Diamond albums in the United States?

Answers

694) Public Enemy

695) Dolly Parton

696) Staind

697) Jake Owen

698) Justin Timberlake

699) Nick*

700) Shania Twain

*Jonas married Priyanka Chopra, winner of the 2000 Miss World Pageant, and the highest paid actress in India.

701. Electronic music producer and DJ "Marshmello" performed a virtual concert inside an online game that was seen by over ten million gamers. What is the name of the video game in which he performed?

702. What band had a top five hit in 2004 with their third single, "She Will Be Loved"?

703. Which rock legend released an album in 2006 titled "Living with War," which was deeply critical of President George W. Bush and his handling of the war in Iraq?

704. What boy band appeared for the first time as a group in 2010 during the seventh season of the British television show "X Factor"?

705. What rapper posthumously released the album "Legends Never Die" In 2020, seven months after his 2019 death by drug overdose?

706. On October 20th, 2018, 84,000 people attended the first concert ever held at Notre Dame Stadium. What legendary country musician performed?

707. What band became only the fourth Canadian act to sell ten million copies of an album when their "All The Right Reasons" went diamond in 2017?

Answers

701) Fortnite

702) Maroon Five

703) Neil Young

704) One Direction

705) Juice WRLD

706) Garth Brooks

707) Nickelback*

The other three to have accomplished this feat are Celine Dion, Shania Twain, and Alanis Morissette.

708. Who paired with Nicki Minaj to perform the song "Barbie World" on the soundtrack to the 2023 film, "Barbie"?

709. Whose 2012 album "The Truth About Love" was her first number one album in the U.S. and contained her fourth number one single, "Just Give Me a Reason"?

710. Who had a top three single in the U.S. in 2012 with his song "Good Feeling" which sampled the Etta James classic "Something's Got a Hold on Me"?

711. Tom Petty married his second wife Dana York in 2001. What original member of the Rock and Roll Hall of Fame officiated the wedding?

712. On December 12, 2012 (12/12/12), a concert was held at Madison Square Garden featuring The Who, Bruce Springsteen, Alicia Keys, Bon Jovi, Billy Joel, Eric Clapton, and many other stars to raise money to provide relief for victims of what hurricane?

713. Name the artist who released a preview of his song "First Class" on TikTok four days before it was released, helping the song debut at number one in 2022?

714. Who appeared on "Glee" on May 4, 2010, to sing her 1981 hit "Physical"?

Answers

708) Ice Spice
709) Pink
710) Flo Rida
711) Little Richard*
712) Sandy
713) Jack Harlow
714) Olivia Newton John

Little Richard also officiated a wedding for Cyndi Lauper, as well as the union of Bruce Willis and Demi Moore.

715. Name the 2000 movie about a saloon which featured four songs by LeAnn Rimes on what would become one of the most popular movie soundtracks of 2000s.

716. What musical superstar did the voice of DJ Suki in the 2016 movie "Trolls"?

717. The only female ever named the Association of Country Music's artist of the decade died on October 4, 2022. Name her.

718. What rapper's album "Recovery" was the best-selling album of 2010?

719. What rocker played the character of Cinna in the "Hunger Games" series"?

720. In 2018, a musical titled "Jagged Little Pill" debuted in Cambridge, Massachusetts. What artist's music was it based on?

721. What Latina artist appeared as a fictionalized version of herself in a 2009 episode of the ABC comedy, "Ugly Betty"?

Answers

715) "Coyote Ugly"
716) Gwen Stefani
717) Loretta Lynn
718) Eminem
719) Lenny Kravitz
720) Alanis Morrisette
721) Shakira

" Jagged Little Pill" was nominated for 15 Tony Awards, the most of any show during the 2019-2020 season. It won two.

722. Who had her only number one hit in the U.S. in 2007 with the song "Girlfriend" from her album "The Best Damn Thing"?

723. As of 2023, who has won more American Music Awards than any other artist?

724. Whose "World's Hottest Tour" was the top grossing tour of 2022?

725. Name the band whose 2020 live version of their song "All Within My Hands" went to number one in September 2020, making them the first band to have number one hits in four decades?

726. Who had their first number one hit in 2002 with "A Moment Like This"?

727. Name the singer of the country anthem "The Devil Went Down to Georgia" who died from a stroke July 6, 2020.

728. Who had their first number one album in 2016 with "Death of a Bachelor"?

Answers

722) Avril Lavigne

723) Taylor Swift*

724) Bad Bunny

725) Metallica

726) Kelly Clarkson

727) Charlie Daniels

728) Panic! at the Disco

*Swift is has won the American Music Award for artist of the year seven times, most of anyone and is also the only artist to win the award three years in a row.

729. Name the band from Omaha, Nebraska led by Conor Oberst who had a top five album with their 2007 release, "Cassadaga."

730. What event annually held each March in Austin, Texas was the first major music festival to announce that it would be cancelled due to the corona virus in March 2020?

731. Name the band led by Thom Yorke who was inducted into the Rock and Roll Hall of Fame in 2019?

732. Name the Grammy Award winning singer and actress who married NFL quarterback Russell Wilson in 2016.

733. In what country was Rihanna born?

734. What country music legend died on his 79th birthday in 2016?

735. What hard rock band released 72 CD recordings from its "Binaural" tour of 2000-2001?

Answers

729) Bright Eyes

730) South by Southwest

731) Radiohead

732) Ciara*

733) Barbados

734) Merle Haggard

735) Pearl Jam

Before her relationship with Wilson, Ciara was engaged and had a child with rapper Future.

736. Who became the first musician to win a Pulitzer Prize in 2008 for his, "profound impact on popular music and American culture"?

737. Which member of OutKast was arrested in Miami in 2011 on drug charges when a container with Viagra and ecstasy in it, labeled with his name, was found in his bag?

738. Name the female music star from Alaska who married Ty Murray, of rodeo fame, in the Bahamas in 2008.

739. Axl Rose, of Guns and Roses, filled in for lead vocalist Brian Johnson during a 2016 tour of what legendary classic rock band?

740. Wiz Khalifa had a number one hit in 2010 with a tribute to his hometown titled "Black and Yellow." What is the name of that town?

741. Name the popular singer songwriter whose hits included "Werewolves of London" and "Lawyers, Guns, and Money" who passed away from cancer in 2003.

742. What singer had a number one country hit in 2000 with "Where I Come From"?

Answers

736) Bob Dylan

737) Big Boi

738) Jewel

739) ACDC

740) Pittsburgh

741) Warren Zevon*

742) Alan Jackson

*David Letterman was a devoted fan of Zevon. When Zevon was diagnosed with terminal lung cancer, and given just a few months to live, he appeared as the only guest on an episode of "The Late Show with David Letterman." Zevon performed three songs, and the two spent the rest of the hour chatting. It was the only time the show featured just one guest.

743. Who won the Grammy for Best Male Pop Vocal Performance in 2003 for "Your Body is a Wonderland"?

744. Who became the first solo female rapper, without a guest artist, to have a number one hit in nearly two decades when her "Bodak Yellow" reached the top of the chart in 2017?

745. What band had their biggest hit in 18 years with their 2022 single "Edging"?

746. In 2020, what rapper competed in season three of "The Masked Singer" as "Robot"?

747. What is the title of the 2014 number one hit by Dierks Bentley for which, in the video of the song, he appears not only as himself, but as the pilot of an airplane?

748. "Lonely Boy" won the Grammy for both Best Rock Performance and Best Rock Song for what band in 2012?

749. What artist made headlines in 2016 when he refused to play a show in North Carolina because of their recently passed law regarding transgender use of bathrooms, causing a wave of other artists to follow suit?

Answers

743) John Mayer

744) Cardi B

745) Blink 182

746) Lil' Wayne

747) "Drunk on a Plane"*

748) The Black Keys

749) Bruce Springsteen

Bentley is, in fact, a licensed pilot.

750. In 2022, what rapper purchased Death Row Records, the label he started with?

751. Name the Albuquerque, New Mexico based band who gained an international audience when their song "New Slang" was featured in the 2004 film, "Garden State."

752. What musician's "Circus Tour" in 2009 grossed over $130 Million, making it one of the highest grossing tours of the decade?

753. Whose 2011 album "Red River Blue" went to the top of the chart, and included the number one singles "Honey Bee," "Drink On It," "Over," and "God Gave Me You"?

754. Name the female British solo artist whose hits include "Love Me Like You Do," "Lights," and "On My Mind."

755. What member of Fleetwood Mac was fired by the rest of the band on April 9, 2018, and replaced by Mike Campbell and Neil Finn for their next tour?

756. What rapper once hosted "MTV Jams" and also played the character of Roman Pearce in the "Fast and Furious" movie series?

Answers

750) Snoop Dogg
752) Britney Spears
754) Ellie Goulding
756) Tyrese Gibson

751) The Shins
753) Blake Shelton
755) Lindsey Buckingham*

*Buckingham alleged that he was fired because bandmate Stevie Nicks gave the band an ultimatum "Either he goes or I go." Nicks has repeatedly denied this.

757. In 2012, who became the youngest male solo artist ever to have a number one country hit, when his song "Wanted" topped the chart while he was 21 years old?

758. The bass player for the Red Hot Chili Peppers was born with the name Michael Balzary. By what one word is he better known?

759. What is the name of the app which debuted in 2008, allowing users to be able to identify song titles and artists simply by holding their phone up and activating the app?

760. What group released their fourth album "3D" six months after member Lisa "Left Eye" Lopes was killed in a car accident?

761. What country music superstar made her film debut in the 2004 film "The Stepford Wives" alongside Nicole Kidman, Matthew Broderick, and Bette Midler?

762. Bobby Hatfield was found dead in his hotel room by his singing partner Bill Medley on November 5, 2003. What was the stage name of this legendary duo?

763. What Mariah Carey song became the first ringtone to achieve certified gold status after selling 500,000 copies?

Answers

757) Hunter Hayes
758) Flea*
759) Shazam
760) TLC
761) Faith Hill
762) The Righteous Brothers
763) "All I Want for Christmas Is You"

Flea has three children, each 17 years apart in age.

764. In 2019, Taylor Swift collaborated with Brendan Urie to score a number one hit with the song "Me!" What band is Urie the lead singer for?

765. Who received three Grammy nominations for their second album "Konvicted" in 2006?

766. What band released their debut album "2 Cool 4 Skool" in 2013?

767. What rap act played their final concert together at Bonnaroo in 2009, shortly before founding member Adam Yauch was diagnosed with cancer?

768. What band had their best-selling hit in 2006 with "Burnin' Up"?

769. "We Don't Talk About Bruno" set the record for longest number one hit from a Disney movie in 2021.
What is the title of the movie in which it was originally featured?

770. On what popular television show did Chris Brown appear in three episodes in 2007 as a band geek named Will Tutt?

Answers

764) Panic! At the Disco   765) Akon
766) BTS   767) The Beastie Boys*
768) Jonas Brothers   769) "Encanto"
770) "The O.C."

*Yauch died within three years of the diagnosis, and the surviving members disbanded, saying there was no Beastie Boys without him.

771. What popular animated television show did 50 Cent appear on in 2005 in an episode titled "Pranksta Rap"?

772. Name the Massachusetts based "Celtic-Punk" band whose song "I'm Shipping Up to Boston" was featured in the 2006 film, "The Departed."

773. Name the singer and actress who in 2011 became a judge for the popular show "American Idol" and was named People Magazine's "Most Beautiful Person" the same year.

774. What legendary musician held a residency at Caesar's Palace in Las Vegas from 2004 to 2009 titled "The Red Piano"?

775. Cory Monteith was found dead in a Vancouver, B.C. hotel room on July 13, 2013. He played a character named Finn Hudson on what popular musical television show?

776. Who, in 2022, became the first female solo artist to have her first seven albums go to number one on the chart?

777. Name the song, popular at weddings, which paired Jason Mraz and Colbie Caillat together and was released in 2009.

Answers

771) "The Simpsons"
773) Jennifer Lopez
775) "Glee"
777) "Lucky"

772) The Dropkick Murphys
774) Elton John*
776) Beyonce

John came back to do another residency at Caesar's Palace from 2011 to 2018, which grossed over $130 million.

778. Give the title to the 2003 Toby Keith song which begins with "We got winners, we got losers, chain smokers and boozers."

779. What hip hop star founded Beats Electronics in 2006?

780. What song by the band Queen was named the "Most streamed classic rock song in history" in 2018?

781. What rapper performed an updated version of his 2009 song "Kobe Bryant" at the BET Awards in 2020 after the basketball star's death?

782. On March 25, 2015, Zayn Malik announced he was leaving what popular boy band?

783. What actress and singer played the role of Sharpay Evans in the "High School Musical" film series?

784. Who released her twelfth studio album "MDNA" in 2012, which became her eighth to reach the top spot on the Billboard Hot 200?

Answers

778) "I Love This Bar"

779) Dr. Dre

780) "Bohemian Rhapsody"

781) Lil' Wayne*   782) One Direction

783) Ashley Tisdale

784) Madonna

*Lil Wayne is a huge Laker fan. On his 2020 album "Funeral," he left 24 seconds of the album silent, as Bryant switched to the jersey number 24 for the latter portion of his career.

785. At the 2002 American Music Awards, who was named "Artist of the Century"?

786. What artist had her third consecutive number one album with her 2007 release, "Not Too Late"?

787. Name the artist who in 2017 accepted the National Equality Award for her work supporting LGBTQ causes and admitted in her acceptance speech that she had done more than just "Kissed a girl."

788. What R and B group spent three weeks at number one in the year 2000 with "Say My Name"?

789. Only three rappers in history have both hosted and been the musical guest on "Saturday Night Live" on the same night. One is MC Hammer, another is Lucacris. Who, in 2014, became the third rapper to achieve this feat?

790. Carrie Underwood married professional athlete Mike Fisher in 2009. What sport did he play?

791. Rivers Cuomo is the lead singer of a band that got its name from a nickname he was called by when he was growing up because of his asthma. What is the band's name?

Answers

785) Michael Jackson

786) Norah Jones

787) Katy Perry

788) Destiny's Child

789) Drake*

790) Hockey

791) Weezer

*As of September 2023, 44 artists have been both the musical guest and host of SNL. Paul Simon was the first to do it in 1975 and did it another three times.

792. What legendary performer who was inducted into the Rock and Roll Hall of Fame as both a solo artist and part of a duo passed away on May 24, 2023?

793. Give the title to the song that was a number one hit for Robyn in 2010, and then became a hit for Calum Scott when he did a cover of it in 2016.

794. What former Beatle released their twelfth and final studio album titled "Brainwashed" in 2002?

795. Whose 2006 debut solo album titled "The Dutchess" featured three number one singles?

796. By what name is the rapper born Clifford Joseph Harris, Jr., whose hits include "What You Know" and "Rubber Band Man," better known as?

797. Luke Combs had a number one country hit in 2023 with a cover of what 1988 Tracy Chapman song?

798. Who, at the age of 18, became the youngest artist ever to win the MTV Video Music Award song of the year in 2021?

Answers

792) Tina Turner
794) George Harrison
796) T.I.
798) Olivia Rodrigo

793) "Dancing on My Own"
795) Fergie
797) "Fast Car" *

Chapman became the first African American woman to be the sole songwriter of a number one country hit.

799. What pop superstar portrayed the character Marion Crane in the final season of "Bates Motel" on A and E in 2017?

800. What classic rock group toured in support of their album "Long Road Out of Eden" in 2008?

801. Name the country and gospel singer who had two number one country hits in 2006: "Your Man" and "Would You Go with Me."

802. Who made a surprise appearance at a Red Sox game at Fenway Park in Boston five days after the Boston Marathon bombings of 2013 to sing his classic "Sweet Caroline"?

803. Name the band from Berkley, California who was named the "Greatest Punk Band of All Time" by Rolling Stone Magazine in 2011.

804. What alternative band led by Hayley Williams won the Grammy for Best Rock Song in 2015 for "Ain't it Fun"?

805. Whose 2006 album "Doctor's Advocate," featuring the smash hit "Hate It or Love It," was named the best hip hop album of 2006 by the New York Times?

Answers

799) Rihanna

801) Josh Turner

803) Green Day*

805) The Game

800) The Eagles

802) Neil Diamond

804) Paramore

*This accolade was based on a poll of the magazine's readers. The Clash was second, with the Ramones, Sex Pistols, and Dead Kennedys rounding out the top five.

806. What pop star did film maker and actress Olivia Wilde begin dating in late 2020?

807. What artist rose to international stardom after collaborating with Taylor Swift on the song "Everything Has Changed" in 2012?

808. What Hawaiian born singer, along with friends, performed the soundtrack for the 2006 animated film "Curious George"?

809. What rapper's single "Super Freaky Girl" debuted at number one in 2022, making her the first female rapper to accomplish that feat since Lauryn Hill did it in 1998?

810. What 2015 movie soundtrack featured songs by Ella Goulding, The Weeknd, Shawn Mendes, and Charlie Puth while becoming the seventh best-selling album of that year?

811. What British female singer had a number one hit in 40 countries with her 2001 release "Can't Get You Out of My Head"?

812. What female singer was, in 2020, named by Billboard Magazine: "The Greatest Music Video Artist of All Time"?

Answers

806) Harry Styles

807) Ed Sheeran

808) Jack Johnson

809) Nicki Minaj

810) "50 Shades of Grey"

811) Kylie Minogue

812) Madonna*

Michael Jackson was second, followed by Beyonce, Janet Jackson, and Missy Elliot.

813. Whose album "Born and Raised" had to be pushed back because he had throat surgery performed?

814. Who became the first K-pop all female group to have a number one hit in the United States, with their second album "Born Pink" in 2020?

815. Whose song "Watching You" was the number one selling country single of 2007?

816. In what popular NBC drama did singer Mandy Moore play the role of Rebecca Pearson from 2016 to 2022?

817. What legendary musician played the last show of his "Homeward Bound Farewell Tour" in New York City in 2018, just a few miles from where he grew up?

818. Who did Billboard Magazine name the top Latin artist for back to back decades, the 2000s and the 2010s?

819. What country and pop superstar released the album "Now" in 2017, her first studio album in 15 years?

Answers

813) John Mayer
815) Rodney Atkins
817) Paul Simon
819) Shania Twain*

814) Blackpink
816) "This is Us"
818) Shakira

Twain did not perform for nearly a decade after she lost her voice, and suffered vocal cord damage due to Lyme disease, her doctors believe.

820. In what year did Spotify make its debut?

821. The album "Raising Sand" won the Grammy for "Album of the Year" in 2009. It was a collection of duets between Alison Kraus and what iconic rock frontman?

822. What country music star began hosting a Sunday morning show on the Food Network in 2018, after she had already released two cookbooks?

823. Name the rock star who has been inducted into the Rock and Roll Hall of Fame as a part of two different bands who released his autobiography titled "The Storyteller: Tales of Life and Music" in 2021.

824. What fellow cannabis lover joined Snoop Dogg for their 2016 tour known as "The High Road" tour?

825. In 2001, what country legend left the hospital after being treated for pneumonia to go to the Grammy Awards where he won his tenth, this time for Best Male Vocal Country Performance for "Solitary Man"?

826. In 2009, A.R. Rahman won Academy Awards for Best Original Score and Best Song for the song "Jai Ho." What movie was it from?

Answers

820) 2008

821) Robert Plant*

822) Martina McBride

823) Dave Grohl

824) Wiz Khalifa

825) Johnny Cash

826) "Slumdog Millionaire"

*Alison Kraus once held the record for most Grammy wins by a female, until she was surpassed by Beyonce.

827. Name the singer and actress who first broke into the spotlight by playing Lizzie McGuire and later had a number one album titled "Metamorphosis."

828. Songs by Willie Nelson, Chris Stapelton, Jason Isbell, Ryan Bingham, and many others can be found on the soundtrack to what popular series starring Kevin Costner which premiered in 2018?

829. Name the singer, songwriter, and guitarist who wrote the classics "The Weight," "Up on Cripple Creek," and "The Night They Drove Old Dixie Down" who passed away in Los Angeles in 2023.

830. What rapper was banned from performing in the United Kingdom in 2015 because they determined that lyrics in his albums "Bastard" and "Goblin" incited terrorism?

831. Name the band whose 2008 video "Pork and Beans" featured a compilation of popular YouTube stars of the time.

832. What actor topped the R and B / Hip Hop chart for 14 consecutive weeks with his 2008 hit "Blame It (On the Alcohol)"?

833. Who won "Song of the Year" at the 2018 Grammy Awards for his "That's What I Like"?

Answers

827) Hilary Duff

828) "Yellowstone"

829) Robbie Robertson *

830) Tyler, the Creator

831) Weezer

832) Jamie Foxx

833) Bruno Mars

Robertson collaborated on many movie soundtracks and scores with Martin Scorsese, including "Raging Bull," "The King of Comedy," and "Casino."

834. What group's song "Sugar" spent 20 weeks in the top ten in 2015?

835. Who rented out the entire Staples Center in Los Angeles in 2011 so that he and his girlfriend Selena Gomez could have a private viewing of the movie "Titanic" in the 20,000-seat arena?

836. Of the bands in the Rock and Roll Hall of Fame, the first in alphabetical order was inducted in 2010. Name it.

837. What song written by Ryan Adams was turned into a 21st century hit for The Corrs, featuring Bono, and later for Tim McGraw?

838. Name the actress who once dated John F. Kennedy Jr, had a long-term relationship with Jackson Browne, and married rock legend Neil Young in 2018.

839. Whose song "Havana" was the best-selling song in the world in 2018?

840. In 2017, a star studded farewell tribute to what retiring music legend closed with him singing a duet with Dolly Parton for their classic "Islands in the Stream"?

Answers

834) Maroon Five

835) Justin Bieber

836) Abba

837) "Where the Stars Go Blue"

838) Daryl Hannah

839) Camila Cabello

840) Kenny Rogers*

*"Islands in the Stream" was originally written by the Bee Gees, and draws its name from a novel by Ernest Hemmingway, which was the first of his works to be released after his death.

841. Whose 2017 self-titled debut album is the most streamed album by a female artist in the history of Spotify?

842. What rapper had his first number one album with his 2003 release "Chicken-N-Beer"?

843. What superstar female singer played a character named Skye Summers for two episodes in the hip-hop centered television series, "Atlanta" in 2015?

844. Name the satirical dark comedy horror series on the Fox Network which aired for two seasons starting in 2015 and featured both Nick Jonas and Ariana Grande in recurring roles?

845. Name the entrepreneur and British music executive who was the first executive producer of "America's Got Talent"?

846. Name the animated series which appeared on MTV from 1993 to 1997, was brought back in 2011, and returned again on Paramount in 2022?

847. What member of the Wu Tang Clan was arrested November 27, 2000 after escaping from a drug-rehabilitation center?

Answers

841) Dua Lipa

842) Ludacris

843) Alicia Keys

844) "Scream Queens"

845) Simon Cowell

846) "Beavis and Butthead"

847) Old Dirty Bastard*

After escaping from the rehab center in Los Angeles, O.D.B. briefly performed with Wu Tang Clan in New York City, then was arrested in Philadelphia when recognized at a McDonald's drive through window.

848. What band's top ten hit from 2009 "Good Life" featured cameos by Nicolas Cage, Anne Hathaway, and Russell Crowe in its music video?

849. What 2002 movie starring Taye Diggs and Sanaa Lathan about a couple who fall in love through hip-hop music has a soundtrack featuring Kanye West, Mos Def, Erykah Badu, and Common?

850. What singer announced that they were non-binary during a 2019 interview on an Instagram series hosted by actress Jameela Jamil?

851. What former member of the Fugees was arrested and handcuffed by Los Angeles Police after he was mistaken for a robbery suspect near where he was recording?

852. What rap duo won the Grammy for "Best Rap Album" in 2014 for "The Heist"?

853. What country music star became the second musician ever to be named People Magazine's "Sexiest Man Alive" in 2017?

854. What actor won an Oscar for his portrayal of Ray Charles in the 2005 movie, "Ray"?

Answers

848) One Republic*
850) Sam Smith
852) Macklemore and Ryan Lewis
854) Jamie Foxx

849) "Brown Sugar"
851) Wyclef Jean
853) Blake Shelton

*The song had a very long shelf life, peaking at number 8 two years after its release due to its use in several movies and television shows, including "Eat, Pray, Love," "Gossip Girl," and "One Tree Hill."

855. Name the title to the 2001 Grammy Winning single by the Dave Matthews Band which begins with "You Cannot quit me so quickly. There's no hope in you for me. No corner you could squeeze me, but I got all the time for you, love."

856. Who won the award for "Top Rap Song" at the 2018 Billboard Music Awards for "Rockstar"?

857. Questlove performed the voice for the character Curly in what 2020 Pixar film?

858. What country music legend starred in the lead role of the Broadway Production of "Annie Get Your Gun" for five months in 2001?

859. What pop star appeared dressed as a cheeseburger in Taylor Swift's 2019 video, "You Need to Calm Down"?

860. Who, in 2020, became the youngest artist to record the theme song to a James Bond movie?

861. Who had a number one country hit in 2004 with the title track to his album "Mud On the Tires"?

Answers

855) "Space Between Us"   856) Post Malone
857) "Soul"   858) Reba McEntire
859) Katy Perry*   860) Billie Eilish
861) Brad Paisley

*Perry's appearance in the video marked the end of a six year feud between the two stars, which included accusations of stealing back-up dancers and subtle jabs in songs at each other.

862. What female solo artist is also a member of the groups Boygenius and Better Oblivion Community Center?

863. Who, in 2013, became the first artist to have five number one albums before turning 19 years old?

864. What Michigan born singer had a top ten hit in 2010 with "Cooler Than Me" and another in 2015 with "I Took a Pill in Ibiza"?

865. Who became the first African woman to headline the Coachella Music Festival in 2018?

866. What Los Angeles based band won the 2020 Grammy for Best Metal Performance for their song "7empest," which is over 15 minutes long?

867. What singer, who also starred in the film "Hidden Figures," had a best-selling album in 2018 titled "Dirty Computer"?

868. Name the country music star who released his debut album titled "American Heartbreak" in 2022, after he finished eight years of service for the United States Navy?

Answers

862) Phoebe Bridgers.
864) Mike Posner
866) Tool
868) Zach Bryan

863) Justin Bieber
865) Beyonce*
867) Janelle Monae

Beyonce's performance is the most viewed on YouTube in the history of the festival.

869. What country is the singer known as "Sia" from?

870. When founding member of The Eagles, Glen Frey, passed away in 2016, fans left flowers and gifts for him at his statue in "Standing on the Corner Park" in which city?

871. Give the title of a 2022 hit song by Ed Sheeran and Fireboy DML which is also the name of a country in South America.

872. What country music star earned critical acclaim for his role as an alcoholic father in the 2004 film "Friday Night Lights"?

873. What hard rocking Australian band had a number one album with their 17th release, "Power Up" in 2020?

874. Fatboy Slim won the 2002 Grammy for Best Music Video for his "Weapon of Choice." What famous actor is featured dancing around a deserted hotel lobby in it?

875. In 2006, what artist released an album titled "The Seeger Sessions" which consisted entirely of covers of songs by folk legend Pete Seeger?

Answers

869) Australia

870) Winslow, Arizona*

871) Peru

872) Tim McGraw

873) AC/DC

874) Christopher Walken

875) Bruce Springsteen

Taken from the Eagles classic "Take it Easy," Standing on the Corner Park in Winslow Arizona features a flatbed Ford and they constantly play Eagles songs over loud speakers.

876. What famous rock band leader released the soundtrack to the 2007 movie "Into the Wild" as his first album as a solo artist?

877. Name the Scottish DJ who topped Forbes Magazine's list of the world's highest paid DJs each year from 2013 to 2018?

878. Name the artist nicknamed The King of Punk-Funk who returned to the cultural spotlight in America after being satirized on the "Chappelle Show."

879. In 2009, nearly 14,000 people set a world record by joining together to dance to what Michael Jackson song on what would have been his 51st birthday?

880. Name the son of another music legend who holds the record for most number one songs on the Hot Latin Chart, with 27.

881. What band won the Grammy Award for "Best Rock Song" for their 2000 release "With Arms Wide Open"?

882. What legendary band consisting of Neil Young, Stephen Stills, and Richie Furay reunited for seven shows in 2011, including a performance at Bonnaroo?

Answers

876) Eddie Vedder

877) Calvin Harris

878) Rick James*

879) "Thriller"

880) Enrique Iglesias

881) Creed

882) Buffalo Springfield

The recurring skit of Chappelle imitating Rick James was so popular it was nearly turned into a movie.

883. What hip hop star released the album "4:44" in 2017 which addressed accusations of infidelity against his wife, who is also a star?

884. What classic rock band toured with Adam Levine as their lead singer in 2012?

885. What female superstar wrapped up her "Living Proof" tour in 2005, which was the highest grossing tour by a female in history at that point?

886. Whose 2000 album "The Marshall Mathers LP" sold 1.76 copies in the first week, making it the fastest selling rap album in history?

887. What female country music legend from Kentucky was awarded the Presidential Medal of Freedom by President Brack Obama in 2013?

888. On October 1, 2017, all tickets for a reunion concert by an all-female band sold out 38 seconds after they went on sale. Name that band.

889. Who released her debut album "Music of the Sun" in 2005 at the age of 17?

Answers

883) Jay-Z

884) Queen

885) Cher*

886) Eminem

887) Loretta Lynn

888) The Spice Girls

889) Rihanna

Cher's record was broken by Madonna in 2009, which was broken by Taylor Swift's "Eras" tour in 2023.

890. Which sport began using Green Day's song "Fire, Ready, Aim" as the opener to their Wednesday night television broadcasts.

891. Which female singer became the first to debut a country song on twitter when she did so in 2012 with "American Heart"?

892. Name the 2015 hit by The Weeknd which begins with, "And I know she'll be the death of me, at least we'll both be numb."

893. Whose 2021 single "Go Easy on Me" was written about going through a divorce with her husband, Simon Konecki?

894. What singer/actress released her debut album "Don't Forget" in 2008, which debuted at number two on the Billboard album chart?

895. What popular boy band which included brothers Nick and Drew Lachey reunited in 2017 to record a Christmas album titled "Let it Snow"?

896. What female artist had their first number one hit in 2020 with "Savage"?

Answers

890) Hockey

891) Faith Hill

892) "Can't Feel My Face"?

893) Adele

894) Demi Lovato

895) 98 Degrees

896) Megan Thee Stallion*

*Born with the name Megan Jovan Ruth Peete, she took on the name "The Stallion" because of her large, strong physical stature. She says that strong bodied women in the south are often referred to as "stallions."

897. John Rzeznik was inducted into the songwriter's hall of fame in 2008. What band has been the lead singer of since 1986?

898. What is the name of the 2018 song by Bad Bunny, Cardi B, and J Balvin which was named The Best Summer Song of All Time by Rolling Stone magazine?

899. Who had a number one country album in 2020 with "The Speed of Now, Part One"?

900. What basketball hall of famer is also a 21st century rapper who goes by the stage name "DJ Diesel"?

901. What video game released a version which featured members of the band Green Day dressed as pigs?

902. In 2016, the band Little Big Town had a hit with "Better Man." What superstar wrote the song?

903. What artist revealed in 2017 that she had a kidney transplant because of her battle with lupus, in which she had a kidney donated by good friend Francia Raisa?

Answers

897) The Goo Goo Dolls
899) Keith Urban
901) "Angry Birds"
903) Selana Gomez*

898) "I Like It"
900) Shaquille O'Neal
902) Taylor Swift

*Raisa, an actress, and Gomez became very close friends after meeting each other on a Disney-ABC mandated trip to visit a children's hospital.

904. What singing superstar was appointed to be an ambassador for her native country of Barbados in 2018?

905. Whose album "Handwritten" debuted at number one, making him one of only five artists to ever debut atop the Billboard album chart prior to turning eighteen years old?

906. What music legend released an album of ABBA covers in 2018 called "Dancing Queen" which topped the chart in 19 countries?

907. Whose song "Low" was named the Billboard Song of the Year in 2008?

908. What pop superstar married actor Russel Brand in 2010?

909. Name the 2022 movie in which Harry Styles plays the character Jack Chambers.

910. What rapper got into an fist fight with Frank Ocean in outside of an L.A. recording studio, allegedly over a parking spot in 2013?

Answers

904) Rihanna

905) Shawn Mendes*

906) Cher

907) Flo Rida

908) Katy Perry

909) "Don't Worry Darling"

910) Chris Brown

*Justin Bieber, Miley Cyrus, Hilary Duff, and LeAnn Rimes each had two number one albums before they turned eighteen.

911. What song by Glass Animals broke the record for most weeks in the Billboard Top 100, at 91 in September 2022?

912. BTS made their first appearance on the "Tonight" show in 2020 when they performed their song "On" from what New York City location, which has nearly a million visitors every day?

913. Name the Puerto Rican music star who played the role of Antonio D'Amico in the 2010 series "The Assassination of Gianni Versace: American Crime Story."

914. What country music legend made an appearance as an angel in the last episode of the series "Grace and Frankie" in 2022?

915. Name the all-female group, popular in the 1980s, who played their final show together in 2016 at the Greek Theater in Los Angeles.

916. Name the pop star from New Zealand who released her third solo album titled "Solar Power" in 2021?

917. The term "bro-country" appears for the first time in New York Magazine to describe the song "Cruise" by the Florida Georgia Line. Which country music star does the author say is the king of the genre?

Answers

911) "Heat Waves"
913) Ricky Martin
915) The Go-Go's
917) Luke Bryan

912) Grand Central Station*
914) Dolly Parton
916) Lorde

The band filmed the video during the restrictions caused by the covid-19 pandemic by having neighbors film the video using their phones.

918. In 2011, what artist became the third in history to have number one singles in three different decades when her "Hold it Against Me" topped the chart?

919. In 2021, an ABC television series starring Brandy and Eve as members of a hip-hop group from the 1990s who get back together in the 2020s. Name that show.

920. What rapper thanked himself in his speech following getting a star on the Hollywood Walk of Fame, which inspired the title track to his next album, "I Wanna Thank Me"?

921. What pop superstar made her acting debut in the 2013 film "Machete Kills"?

922. What highly successful 21st century metal band has a mascot simply known as "The Guy"?

923. What popular entertainer became a Saturday Night Live legend with skits including "Motherlover," "Immigrant Tale," and "Target Lady"?

924. What legendary classic rock band released a compilation of greatest hits in 2012 titled "GRRR!"?

Answers

918) Britney Spears

919) "Queens"

920) Snoop Dogg

921) Lady Gaga

922) Disturbed

923) Justin Timberlake*

924) The Rolling Stones

*Timberlake has won four Emmy awards for his work on the show. Two for Outstanding Guest Actor in a Comedy Series and two for Outstanding Original Music and Lyrics.

925. Who won the Grammy for both Artist of the Year and Album of the Year for in 2005 for her work titled "The Emancipation of Mimi"?

926. Name the male singer who finished second to Ruben Stoddard on the second season of "American Idol" in 2003 and would later run unsuccessfully in 2014 and 2022 to represent North Carolina in the U.S. House of Representatives.

927. What country music singer had a number one album with his eighth studio release, titled "Scarecrow" in 2001?

928. What English female singer had her third chart-topping album in the U.K. in 2020 with "Brightest Blue"?

929. Who joined George Strait to cover "Murder on Music Row," which would win the CMA for "Song of the Year" in 2001?

930. What viral video and dance craze hit by the DJ and producer known as Baauer stayed at number one for five weeks in 2013 on the Billboard Hot 100 chart?

931. Name the Canadian rock legend who recorded the song "Let's Roll" in 2002 to those who died while overtaking United Flight 93 on September 11, 2001?

Answers

925) Mariah Carey

926) Clay Aiken

927) Garth Brooks

928) Ellie Goulding

929) Alan Jackson

930) "Harlem Shake"

931) Neil Young

One of the leaders of the passenger revolt was Todd Beamer. His signal to begin the attack on the hijackers was him saying "Let's Roll." The phrase became a battle cry for American forces in the war on terror.

932. Who had her 18th number one hit in the United States in 2008, surpassing Elvis Presley's previous record of 17.

933. Name the singer, well known for his sexy and sultry soul music, who died of kidney failure at the age of 58 in 2008.

934. What rapper had a number one album in 2000 with "Rule 3:36" and another in 2001 with "Pain is Love"?

935. Who was named by Forbes magazine as the world's wealthiest female musician in 2021, with a net worth of over $1.7 billion?

936. Name the female pop superstar who, in 2011, became the first artist in history to have a single (not the same one) in the Billboard top ten for 52 straight weeks?

937. What band, led by Michael Stipe, played their final performance together in Mexico City in 2008?

938. Name the country music star who played Robby Ray Stewart in the sitcom "Hannah Montana" from 2006 to 2011?

Answers

932) Mariah Carey
934) Ja Rule
936) Katy Perry *
938) Billy Ray Cyrus

933) Barry White
935) Rihanna
937) R.E.M.

Swedish pop group Ace of Base previously held the record, with 48 consecutive weeks in the top ten.

939. What band topped the pop chart for the first time with "Dynamite" on September 5, 2020?

940. Name the "Margaritaville" singer who passed away due a rare and aggressive form of skin cancer on September 1, 2023.

941. What rapper, with help from Ludacris, had a top 40 hit in 2002 with "Welcome to Atlanta"?

942. What band had each of their first seven albums reach number one in the U.K., including "Sam's Town," "Day and Age," and "Battle Born"?

943. Name the singer and actress who had a top five hit in 2002 with her debut single, "Pieces of Me."

944. What classic rock band provided the themes song for "C.S.I.: Crime Scene Investigation" when it premiered on October 5, 2000?

945. Name the rapper known for his eccentric haircut, positive outlook, and was nominated for a Grammy for his work on the song "Broccoli" in 2016.

Answers

939) BTS
941) Jermaine Dupri*
943) Ashlee Simpson
945) Lil Yachty

940) Jimmy Buffett
942) The Killers
944) The Who

The song also features Ludacris. Both he and Dupri are from Atlanta. Ludacris put the song on his second album "Word of Mouf" as a hidden track.

946. What British Grammy Award winning singer was married to supermodel Heidi Clum from 2005 to 2014?

947. What band had a big hit in 2004 joining country and rap in the song "Save a Horse (Ride a Cowboy)"?

948. Name the 2003 Romantic comedy starring pop superstar Jennifer Lopez that is often panned as "one of the worst movies of all time"

949. What classic rock legend had a recurring role as the voice of the character Lucky Kleinschmidt in the animated series "King of the Hill" from 2004 to 2009?

950. Name the singer of country hit "Guys Do It All the Time" who died by suicide in 2013.

951. Name the group whose single "Tongue Tied" was featured in a commercial series for Apple in 2011.

952. After performing together for over three decades, what band, led by Dave Mustaine, won its first Grammy in 2017 for its song "Dystopia"?

Answers

946) Seal

947) Big and Rich

948) "Gigli"

949) Tom Petty

950) Mindy McReady

951) Grouplove

952) Megadeath*

*Mustaine was an original member of Motley Crue, but was fired by the rest of the band due to his excessive drinking and angry demeanor because of it. He had already written several songs which would appear on Motley Crue's debut album.

953. The Museum of Pop Culture, also known as MoPop opened in the year 2000 in what American city, originally being called the Experience Music Project?

954. What Disney channel series featuring Selena Gomez did Shakira make a surprise appearance on in 2010?

955. What reality television star married Blink 182 drummer Travis Barker in 2022?

956. In May 2015, what female superstar's song Ghosttown reached number one on the dance music chart, giving her the most number ones of any kind of any artist in history?

957. What duo had a number one country hit in 2018 with "Speechless"?

958. Name the English rock band who won the Grammy for Best Album for "Drones" in 2016, which was its fifth straight album to top the charts in the U.K.

959. Who became the first artist in three years to sell more than a million copies of an album in a single week with his 2008 release "Tha Carter III"?

Answers

953) Seattle

954) "Wizards of Waverly Place"

955) Kourtney Kardashian

956) Madonna

957) Dan and Shay

958) Muse

959) Lil Wayne*

*50 Cent was the last artist prior to Lil Wayne to accomplish the feat. In total (as of September 2023) there have been 20 albums which have sold a million copies in a week.

960. What series about the truths and untruths of online dating premiered on MTV on November 12, 2012?

961. What Bob Seger song did Chevy stop using its commercials in 2004, ending a 15-year campaign?

962. Who became only the fifth artist in history to replace themselves in the number one spot on the singles chart when his "Dilemma" took the top spot from "Hot in Herre" in 2002?

963. According to an article released by Billboard Magazine in 2022, who is the most Shazamed artist of all time?

964. What country music superstar divorced his wife Sandy Mahl in 2001, with whom he had three daughters?

965. What member of legendary rock group Kiss was fired by Donald Trump during the third season of "The Apprentice" in 2008?

966. What Miami born artist trademarked his famous grito (traditional Mexican shout) in 2019?

Answers

960) "Catfish: The TV Show" 961) "Like a Rock"
962) Nelly 963) Drake
964) Garth Brooks 965) Gene Simmons
966) Pitbull*

There are over 2.6 million patents in the United States, Pitbull's was only the 26th for a sound.

967. What band demanded that Presidential candidate Donald Trump stop using their song "My Hero" during in 2015?

968. What iconic British rocker welcomed his eighth child into the world in 2016 at the age of 73, with his girlfriend Melanie Hamrick?

969. Name the founding member of the hard rock group Sleater-Kinney who was nominated for an Emmy nine times for her work on the series "Portlandia."

970. What young country music star sued her father and her former manager in 2000, claiming they had stolen over $12 million from her?

971. In 2021, Snoop Dogg, Dr. Dre, Kendrick Lamar, Mary J. Blige, and other hip hop stars performed at halftime of the Superbowl. What city was that game held in?

972. Whose "This Is It" tour was to be held in 2011, sold out 50 shows in less than four hours, but never actually happened?

973. What band's song "Blurry" was the top selling rock song of 2002, according to Billboard Magazine?

Answers

967) Foo Fighters

968) Mick Jagger

969) Carrie Brownstein

970) LeAnn Rimes*

971) Los Angeles (Inglewood)

972) Michael Jackson

973) Puddle of Mudd

*Rimes was only 16 at the time she filed the suit against her father, who in turn filed a countersuit. This led to lengthy legal battles, but the two made amends before Rimes's 2002 wedding.

974. What rapper played the character Big Meat in the 2006 action film "Waist Deep"?

975. What Denver based alternative rock band's hits include "Ho Hey" and "Stubborn Love"?

976. What rapper, who gained international fame from his debut album "Come on Over When You're Sober," died of an accidental fentanyl overdose in 2017, just two weeks after his 21st birthday?

977. Name the satirical pop singer who became the first ever guest editor of Mad Magazine in 2015?

978. Rashida Jones, star of "The Office" and "Parks of Recreation," had a baby with Ezra Koenig in 2018. What band is Koenig the lead singer of?

979. Who had a number one single in 2004 with "Goodies" and later went on appear on the cover of the Sports Illustrated Swimsuit Issue?

980. What song by Tones and I is the most streamed song in the history of Spotify by a female artist (as of September 2023)?

Answers

974) The Game

975) The Lumineers

976) Lil' Peep

977) Weird Al Yankovic

978) Vampire Weekend*

979) Ciara

980) "Dance Monkey"

*Jones is also the daughter of legendary music producer Quincy Jones.

981. What rapper, producer, actor, and successful businessman also played in the 2004 season for the American Basketball Association's Las Vegas Rattlers and Long Beach Jam?

982. Who, in 2007, played at Madison Square Garden for the 60th time on his 60th birthday, setting the record for most performances of any artist at that venue?

983. Who had their fifth straight top ten album in 2010 with their album "Bionic"?

984. What rocker had his own highly successful Broadway show in 2017 and 2018, which was reprised in 2021 and turned into a Netflix special?

985. What rock group had back-to-back number one albums in 2005 and 2006 with "Mezmerize" and "Hypnotize" which were recorded during the same session?

986. Name the 17-year-old Canadian whose 2002 debut album "Let Go" went to number one in her native country and sold over seven million copies in the United States.

987. In 2014, the BBC broadcasted "You've Got a Friend" about what legendary female performer?

Answers

981) Master P*

982) Elton John

983) Christina Aguilera

984) Bruce Springsteen

985) System of a Down

986) Avril Lavigne

987) Carole King

In 2022, Master P's net worth was reported at over $200 million, making him one of the richest figures in the hip-hop industry.

988. On June 16th, 2010, four bands who are known simply as the "Big Four" of thrash metal played on the same bill for the first time. Those bands are Anthrax, Megadeth, Metallica, and who?

989. Who became the first female hip hop star inducted into the Rock and Roll Hall of Fame in 2023?

990. What Canadian based coffee and donuts chain paired with Justin Bieber in 2021 to rebrand their donut holes as "Timbiebs"?

991. Nathaniel Dwayne Hale died in 2011 after a series of strokes. By what name was this rapper and cousin of Snoop Dogg better known?

992. What female member of Fleetwood Mac died of a stroke on November 30, 2022?

993. What popular Christmas song was remade by Lydia Liza and Josiah Lemanski in 2016, with the lyrics changed so the singer does not pressure a young lady to spend the night with him?

994. Give the title to the 2016 Billboard Song of the Year by Drake which begins with the lines: "Baby, I like your style. Grips on your waist, front way, back way. You know that I don't play."

Answers

988) Slayer

989) Missy Elliot

990) Tim Hortons

991) Nate Dogg

992) Christine McVie

993) "Baby It's Cold Outside"*

994) "One Dance"

*The song, and its meaning, became a hotly debated issue during the height of the #Metoo movement.

995. In 2022, who had their first number one single in 14 years with "Break My Soul" in 2022?

996. Who had a number one country single in 2017 with the song "Hurricane" from his debut album "This One's for You," which also reached number one on the country album chart?

997. Who won the Grammy for "Best Country Solo Performance" in 2019 for "All Your'n"?

998. What rapper and two-time Grammy winner won the first season of "The Masked Singer" while appearing as "The Monster"?

999. Who paired with Jay-Z to release the single "Umbrella" in 2007, which stayed at number one for seven weeks?

1000. The 2008 movie "Mamma Mia" is based on the songs of what European pop group?

Answers

995) Beyonce

996) Luke Combs

997) Tyler Childers

998) T-Pain*

999) Rihanna

1000) Abba

*T-Pain suffered from depression after being told by Usher that he had "F-ed up music" by using auto tune, so his victory on "The Masked Singer" was especially redeeming.

Please support "Timeless Trivia" by:

1. Leaving a positive review on Amazon.

2. Sharing the link to purchase the "Timeless Trivia" series from Amazon on your own social media.

3. Follow "Timeless Trivia" on Facebook and Instagram.

4. Purchasing one of the other eight books in the "Timeless Trivia" Series available on Amazon.

Coming in March, 2024:

"Timeless Trivia Volume Ten: Sports Trivia of the 1950s, 60s, and 70s"